THE *Ultimate* COOKIE BOOK

Classic, updated & all-new cookie & pastry recipes

CRESTLINE

This edition published in 2010 by
CRESTLINE
A division of BOOK SALES, INC.
276 Fifth Avenue Suite 206
New York, New York 10001
USA

This edition published by arrangement with Creative Publishing International, Inc.

Copyright © 1994 Creative Publishing International, Inc.
400 1ˢᵗ Avenue North Suite 300
Minneapolis, MN 55401
1-800-328-3895
www.creativepub.com

President/CEO: Michael Eleftheriou
Vice President/Publisher: Linda Ball
Vice President /Retail Sales & Marketing: Kevin Haas

Originally published as COOKIES!
Created by: The Editors of Creative Publishing International, Inc.

Test Kitchen Supervisor: Ellen Meis
Home Economists: Ellen Meis, Mary Kaye Sahli, Elizabeth Shedd
Senior Art Director: Delores Swanson
Art Directors: Mark Jacobson, Linda Schloegel
Senior Project Manager: Joseph Cella
Assistant Project Manager: Tracey Stanley
Editor: Janice Cauley
V.P. Development Planning & Production: Jim Bindas
Production Manager: Amelia Merz
Senior Desktop Publishing Specialist: Joe Fahey
Director of Photography: Mike Parker
Creative Photo Coordinator: Cathleen Shannon
Studio Manager: Marcia Chambers
Lead Photographer: Mike Parker
Photographers: Rebecca Hawthorne, Rex Irmen, Bill Lindner
    Mark Macemon, Paul Najlis, Charles Nields
Food Stylists: Bobbette Destiche, Beth Emmons, Nancy Johnson
    Abigail Wyckoff
Production Staff: Kevin Heddin, Mike Hehner, Robert Powers,
    Mike Schauer, Nik Wogstad
Consultants: Johanna Burkhard, Mary Kay Sahli, Grace Wells

ISBN-13: 978-0-7858-2622-4
ISBN-10: 0-7858-2622-X

Printed in China

Contents

Introduction

Food fads come and go, but the popularity of cookies is unchanging. Although we don't know for sure where the first cookie came from, we do know that early cookies were actually tiny cakes that were baked as a test to make sure the oven temperature was right for baking a cake. The name cookie comes from the Dutch word koekje, or "little cake," and the dictionary defines cookies as "small, flat, sweet cakes eaten as snacks or desserts." Today, cookies include a variety of hand-held treats that are enjoyed by young and old alike.

Many cookies familiar to North Americans originated elsewhere. For example, shortbread is a favorite from Scotland, gingersnaps came from Sweden and almond macaroons were first served in Italy. And cookies aren't always called cookies. In Britain, Australia and New Zealand, they are "biscuits" and in Germany, *keks*. Some countries don't even have cookies as we know them, but serve confections that are a cross between cookies and candy.

In this book, you'll find a selection of 200 cookie recipes. There are classic recipes, heirloom favorites and many contemporary treats to entice you. We've even included a chapter on bars and brownies, since they meet our definition of "hand-held treats."

The key to successful cookie making is a thorough understanding of equipment, ingredients and techniques, so we've included some guidelines to get you started. Clear how-to directions and photographs throughout the book will acquaint you with some of the more unusual cookie-making techniques. So whether you're a novice or a seasoned baker, you'll enjoy making the recipes in this collection.

Introduction

5

Equipment

Here is a list of items that will help you make great cookies. Check individual recipes before you start, to be sure you have the required equipment on hand.

Mixing Equipment

Mixing bowls (a): You'll need small, medium and large mixing bowls. They can be glass, heavy plastic or stainless steel.

Measuring cups (b) and Spoons (c): Use standard measuring cups and spoons. For measuring dry ingredients, use dry-measure cups. For liquids, use Pyrex® measuring cups.

Pastry blender (d): Pastry blenders are used to cut shortening into a flour mixture. When the shortening is evenly distributed, the mixture should resemble coarse crumbs.

Electric mixer (e): Hand or upright mixers may be used to mix cookie dough, unless the dough is very firm.

Wooden spoons (f): Use a wooden spoon to mix stiff dough and for general mixing.

Cookie-forming Equipment

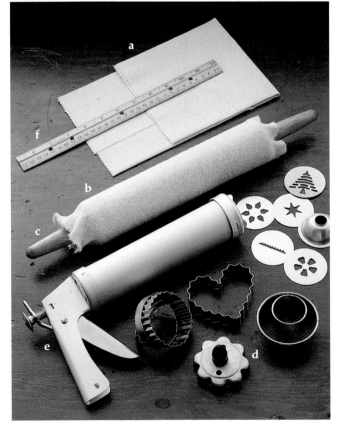

Pastry cloth (a) and Stockinette (b): Dough sticks less when rolled on a pastry cloth than when rolled directly on a floured counter. A cloth stockinette fits over the rolling pin and helps keep dough from sticking to the rolling pin.

Rolling pin (c): Rolling pins are used for rolling out cookie dough.

Cookie cutters (d): Cookie cutters are available in many shapes and sizes. They should be sharp, with no rough edges.

Cookie press (e): This metal, tube-shaped utensil forms the dough into different shapes by forcing it out through a variety of patterned disks onto a cookie sheet.

Ruler (f): A 12-inch (30 cm) measure is handy for measuring rolled-out dough or the size of cookies and pans, or for cutting bars accurately.

Baking Equipment

Cookie sheets: You'll need at least two, and preferably three. We recommend cookie sheets with a small rim on one or two sides; however, a baking sheet with four sides may be used.

Shiny, heavy-gauge aluminum (a) or stainless steel cookie sheets with low sides bake cookies most evenly.

Dark cookie sheets (b) absorb more heat and can cause overbrowning of cookie bottoms. Oven temperature can be reduced 25°F (10°C) to compensate for this.

Nonstick cookie sheets (c) work well if the non-stick finish is not too dark. If it is very dark, reduce oven temperature 25°F (10°C), as above.

Insulated cookie sheets (d), made from two layers of aluminum separated by a layer of air, can prevent cookies from becoming too dark on the bottom but may increase baking time. Some cookie doughs may spread more on these sheets.

Oven thermometer: Hang or stand an oven thermometer in the oven so you can check for accurate oven temperature when you bake.

Timer: Exact baking time is important when baking cookies. Always set a timer when you put your cookies in the oven.

Spatulas: Rubber spatulas are used for folding in ingredients or for scraping dough or batter from the sides of the bowl. Use a large metal or plastic spatula to transfer cookies to and from cookie sheets. A small, angled metal spatula is good for removing bars from a pan.

Cooling racks: You'll need at least two large wire racks. Cooling racks are necessary to allow even cooling on all sides of the cookies. Pans of bars can also be set on cooling racks.

Ingredients

Use fresh ingredients when making cookies, for best results. Check expiration dates on products when purchasing them, and mark the current dates on foods as you store them in your pantry.

Although many ingredients are used to make cookies, the following is a list of the basics:

Eggs

Eggs add flavor, richness, moisture and color. They can also contribute to rising. In our recipes, we used Grade A large eggs. Larger eggs can add too much liquid to the dough, and smaller eggs can make your cookies too dry.

Eggs should have clean, unbroken shells. Use eggs cold, directly from the refrigerator. If room-temperature egg whites are called for in a recipe, separate them from yolks while eggs are cold.

Separate eggs by pouring yolk back and forth between shell halves until white separates and falls into bowl below.

Leavening

Leavening ingredients, like baking powder or baking soda, are what make cookies rise.

We recommend double-acting baking powder, since it is more stable than the single-acting type. Double-acting baking powder reacts both in the mixing of wet and dry ingredients and in baking. Single-acting baking powder reacts as soon as it becomes wet in mixing.

Baking soda, also known as bicarbonate of soda, is also used as a leavener in cookies. It must be combined with an acid ingredient, like buttermilk, molasses or yogurt, to create the desired rising.

Baking soda should always be mixed with the other dry ingredients before any liquids are added, for even distribution. The cookies should then be baked immediately.

Flour

Flour provides the strength and the elasticity needed for cookies to rise. All-purpose flour, either bleached or unbleached, produces light, tender cookies. Whole wheat flour can sometimes be substituted for part of the all-purpose flour, but the resulting cookies will have a firmer, denser texture and will not rise as much.

With some cookies, such as drop cookies, a slightly larger amount of flour results in a chewier cookie, but if the amount is increased too much, the cookies may become too dry.

Measure flour by spooning it lightly into a measuring cup, then leveling it off with a flat-edged knife or spatula. It is not necessary to sift flour for the recipes in this book.

Shortenings

Shortening adds flavor, tenderness and moistness to cookies. Butter and regular stick margarine can be used interchangeably in most of these cookie recipes.

For easy measuring, cut off the amount needed from a refrigerated stick of butter or margarine. Softened butter or margarine should be just soft enough to blend well with other ingredients, not melted. If the recipe calls for vegetable shortening, use solid hydrogenated shortening. Vegetable shortening can be measured by packing it into a dry-measure cup with a spoon.

Butter and margarine both provide good flavor and crisp texture to cookies. Vegetable shortening produces a crunchy, more crumbly cookie but adds little flavor.

Recommended shortenings are butter, regular stick margarine, and vegetable shortening. We do not recommend using whipped butter, whipped margarine, tub-style soft margarine, reduced-calorie margarine or liquid margarine for cookie making. Additional air in these products, plus a generally higher water content, may result in thin, flat cookies.

Sugar

Sugar adds sweetness and texture to cookies. Granulated sugar should be dry and free of lumps.

Brown sugar adds a rich flavor to cookies, and either light or dark brown can be used in our recipes. If brown sugar hardens, it may be difficult to incorporate into the dough. To keep it soft, store it in an airtight container. If brown sugar does become hard, heat it in a 250° to 300°F (120° to 150°C) oven for a few minutes; use it immediately, before it rehardens.

Powdered, or confectioners', sugar is finely pulverized granulated sugar with a small amount of cornstarch added. Measure powdered sugar by spooning it lightly into a measuring cup, then leveling it off with a flat-edged knife or spatula.

Measure granulated sugar by spooning it into a measuring cup, then leveling it off with a flat-edged knife or spatula.

Measure brown sugar by firmly packing it into a measuring cup.

Powdered sugar may need to be sifted before measuring, to remove lumps.

Tips

The following tips will help you make cookies with confidence:

•Follow recipes carefully. Do not overmix dough, because cookies may become tough.

•Preheat oven until it reaches the desired temperature.

•Place oven racks in center position.

•Bake one sheet of cookies at a time to provide the best circulation. If two cookie sheets are used at once, leave 1 inch (2.5 cm) of air space on all sides of both sheets.

•Follow individual recipes for greasing cookie sheets and pans. If greasing is required, use a pastry brush to apply a thin coating of solid shortening.

•A soft cookie dough is easily dropped from a spoon, while a firm dough usually needs to be shaped, rolled or pressed.

•Immediately remove cookies from cookie sheets with a metal or plastic spatula, unless the recipe says to do otherwise. Cookies that remain on a sheet too long can harden and stick. If this happens, put the sheet back in the oven for 1 minute to soften cookies.

•Cool cookie sheets between bakings. If dough is placed on hot sheets, cookies may spread too much, resulting in flat cookies.

Use an electric mixer unless dough is very stiff. When a recipe indicates "light and fluffy," the mixture should be airy and a lighter shade of yellow.

Combine the dry ingredients in a separate bowl before adding to the wet ingredients, for even blending. (Procedures may vary for individual recipes.)

Place cookie sheet in oven, allowing at least 2 inches (5 cm) of clearance on all sides for good air circulation.

| Edges are light golden brown | Edges are golden brown | Light golden brown | Golden brown | Set |

Follow doneness tests indicated in the recipes. "Until edges are light golden brown" means the cookies are just beginning to color on the edges. "Until edges are golden brown" means the edges of the cookies have turned a deeper gold. "Until light golden brown" means the cookies have an even light browning over the surface. "Until golden brown" means the cookies have an attractive golden color. "Until set" means that you can touch the cookies in the center and a slight imprint will remain. This test works best for cookies with dark-colored dough.

Storage

Store cookies carefully, following these easy tips:

• Be sure cookies are completely cooled before storing.

• Store frosted cookies after the frosting or glaze is set or dry.

• Store soft and crisp cookies separately, and store different types of cookies in separate containers, so flavors do not mix.

• For longer storage, freeze cookies. Freeze each type of cookie separately in a tightly covered container. Layer frosted or glazed cookies between sheets of wax paper after frosting is set or dry, or freeze these cookies unfrosted, then frost after thawing. Most cookies freeze well and keep for about 6 months.

• Store meringue cookies in a loosely covered container at room temperature. They do not freeze well.

• For food safety, some cookies may need to be refrigerated. Follow directions in individual recipes.

Use tightly covered containers or plastic food-storage bags. When making more than one variety, label packages carefully.

Place sheets of wax paper between layers of cookies, so they will not stick together.

Store crisp cookies in a container with a loose-fitting cover. If the weather is humid, a tight-fitting cover should be used. If crisp cookies become soft, heat them in a 300°F (150°C) oven for 3 to 5 minutes, or until warm.

Store soft, cakelike cookies in a container with a tight-fitting cover. If necessary, freshen soft cookies by placing an apple wedge or a slice of bread, loosely wrapped in wax paper, into the container.

Shaped, Rolled & Refrigerated Cookies

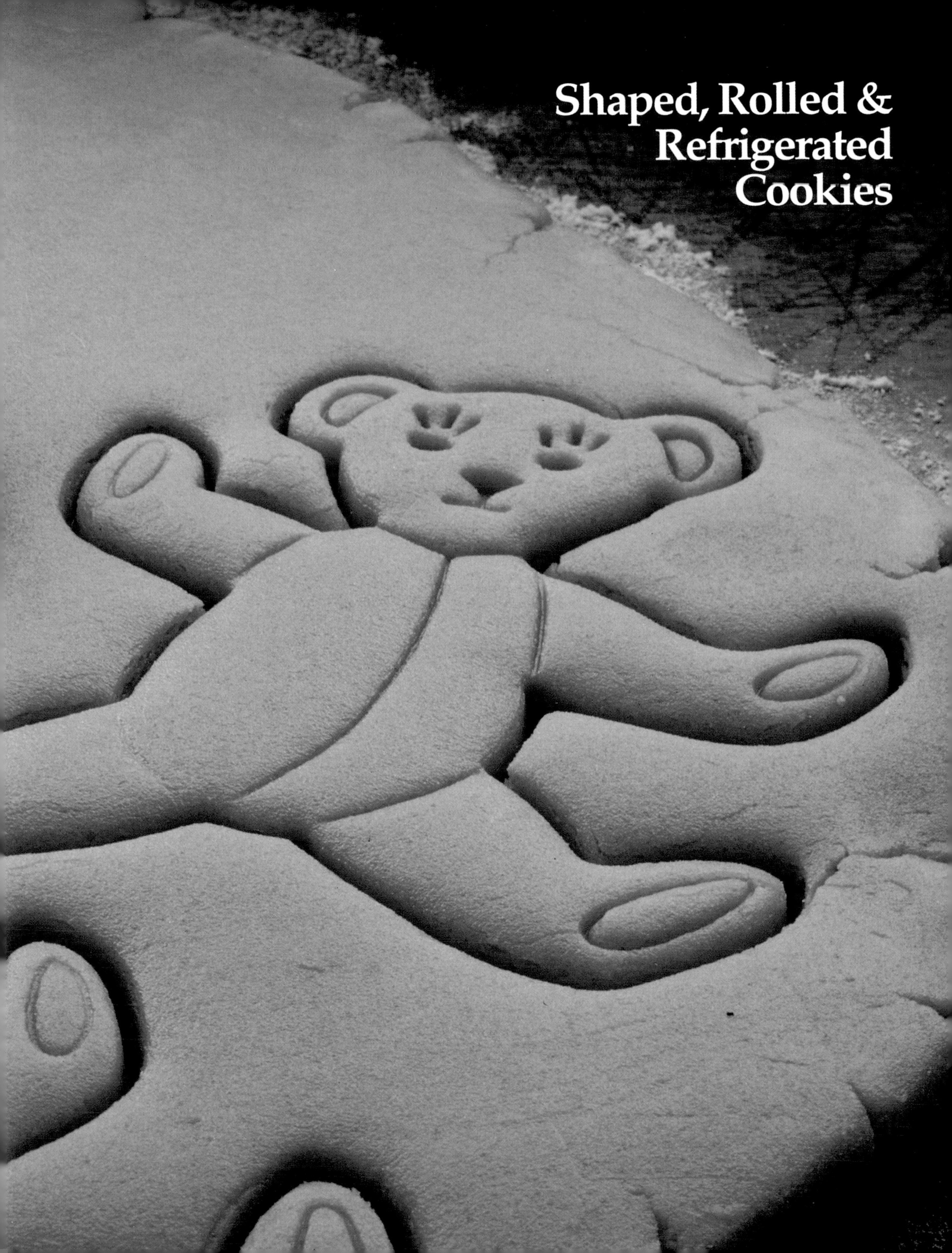

Shaped Cookie Basics

Shaped, or hand molded, cookie dough is shaped into small balls, crescents, logs or other creative designs by hand. Use a spoon to measure out the amount of dough called for in a recipe. For easy handling, refrigerate dough until it is firm and no longer sticky. Dust your hands with a little flour to keep the dough from sticking.

How to Make Shaped Cookies

Form mounds of dough into balls with your hands. Use a ruler to keep the size of cookies consistent.

Follow recipes for specific shaping directions. Shapes other than balls include crescents, logs, S shapes or even pretzels.

Shaped cookies are usually done when the edges and bottoms are golden brown (see page 10). Most shaped cookies should be removed from the cookie sheet immediately after baking to prevent them from sticking to the sheet. Follow individual recipes for doneness tests and removal instructions.

Tips for Making Shaped Cookies

Dip bottom of a glass in sugar and gently press balls of dough on the cookie sheet. Press balls to equal thickness for even baking.

Use glasses with patterned bottoms, if desired, to leave an imprint on the cookies.

Use your imagination to create specialized cookies. Use forks in a criss-cross pattern, patterned backs of spoons, ceramic cookie stamps or other textured items to flatten balls of dough and leave impressions.

Chocolate Almond Logs

  1 *cup (250 mL) sugar*
1/2 *cup (125 mL) plus 1 teaspoon (5 mL) vegetable shortening, divided*
1/2 *cup (125 mL) butter or margarine, softened*
  1 *egg*
  1 *teaspoon (5 mL) almond extract*
2 1/2 *cups (625 mL) all-purpose flour*
1/2 *cup (125 mL) unsweetened cocoa*
1/2 *teaspoon (2 mL) salt*
  1 *cup (250 mL) vanilla baking chips*
  1 *cup (250 mL) chopped almonds*

4 dozen cookies

Heat oven to 375°F (190°C). In large mixing bowl, combine sugar, 1/2 cup (125 mL) shortening, the butter, egg and almond extract. Beat at medium speed of electric mixer until light and fluffy. Add flour, cocoa and salt. Beat at low speed until soft dough forms.

Shape 1 measuring tablespoon (15 mL) dough into 2 1/2-inch (6 cm) log. Repeat with remaining dough. Place logs 2 inches (5 cm) apart on ungreased cookie sheets. Bake for 9 to 12 minutes, or until set. Cool completely.

In 1-quart (1 L) saucepan, combine chips and remaining 1 teaspoon (5 mL) shortening. Melt over low heat, stirring constantly. Dip one end of each log into melted chips, then roll dipped ends in almonds. Place logs on cooling rack or wax paper. Let dry completely before storing.

Microwave tip: In small mixing bowl, melt chips and remaining 1 teaspoon (5 mL) shortening at 50% (Medium) for 2 1/2 to 5 minutes, stirring after every minute. Continue as directed.

Fruit 'n Oat Balls

3 cups (750 mL) uncooked
   old-fashioned rolled oats
1/2 cup (125 mL) flaked coconut
3 tablespoons (50 mL) shelled
   sunflower seeds
1/2 cup (125 mL) sugar
1/2 cup (125 mL) butter or
   margarine
2 eggs, slightly beaten
1/2 cup (125 mL) finely chopped
   dried fruit mix
1/2 to 1 teaspoon (2 to 5 mL)
   almond extract

About 3 dozen cookies

Line airtight container with wax paper. Set aside. In large mixing bowl, combine oats, coconut and seeds. Set aside.

In 1-quart (1 L) saucepan, combine sugar, butter and eggs. Cook over low heat until slightly thickened, stirring constantly. Add dried fruit. Cook until thickened, stirring constantly. Remove from heat. Cool slightly. Stir in almond extract. Pour fruit mixture over oat mixture. Stir until well blended.

While mixture is still warm, shape into 1-inch (2.5 cm) balls. Place balls in prepared container. Store in refrigerator.

Shaped Cookies

Almond Citrus Biscotti

1¹/₂ cups (375 mL) sugar
  ¹/₂ cup (125 mL) unsalted
        butter, softened
    1 teaspoon (5 mL) vanilla
    4 eggs, divided
3³/₄ cups (925 mL) all-purpose
        flour
    1 tablespoon (15 mL) grated
        lemon peel
    2 teaspoons (10 mL) grated
        orange peel
    2 teaspoons (10 mL) baking
        powder
        Pinch of salt
    2 tablespoons (25 mL) coarsely
        ground almonds

3¹/₂ dozen cookies

Heat oven to 350°F (180°C). Lightly grease cookie sheets. Set aside. In large mixing bowl, combine sugar, butter and vanilla. Beat at medium speed of electric mixer until light and fluffy. Add 3 eggs, one at a time, beating after each addition. Add flour, peels, baking powder and salt. Beat at low speed until soft dough forms.

Divide dough into quarters. On lightly floured surface, shape each quarter into 2-inch-diameter (5 cm) log. Place logs 2 inches (5 cm) apart on prepared cookie sheet. Set aside.

In small bowl, lightly beat remaining egg. Brush logs evenly with egg. Sprinkle tops of logs evenly with almonds. Bake for 30 to 35 minutes, or until golden brown. Immediately cut logs diagonally into ³/₄-inch (2 cm) slices. Place slices 1 inch (2.5 cm) apart on prepared cookie sheets. Bake for additional 10 to 15 minutes, or until dry and golden brown. Cool completely before storing.

Maple Crescents

1 cup (250 mL) powdered
  sugar, divided
1 cup (250 mL) unsalted
  butter, softened
1 teaspoon (5 mL) maple extract
1¾ cups (425 mL) all-purpose
  flour
1 cup (250 mL) finely chopped
  pecans
2 to 3 teaspoons (10 to 15 mL)
  milk

3½ dozen cookies

In large mixing bowl, combine ½ cup (125 mL) sugar, the butter and maple extract. Beat at medium speed of electric mixer until light and fluffy. Add flour. Beat at low speed until soft dough forms. Stir in pecans. Cover with plastic wrap. Chill 1 to 2 hours, or until firm.

Heat oven to 350°F (180°C). Shape heaping teaspoons dough into crescent shapes. Place crescents 2 inches (5 cm) apart on ungreased cookie sheets. Bake for 12 to 15 minutes, or until set. Cool completely.

In small mixing bowl, combine remaining ½ cup (125 mL) sugar and the milk. Stir until smooth. Pipe or drizzle glaze over crescents. Let dry completely before storing.

Confetti Peanut Butter Cookies

1/2 cup (125 mL) creamy
    peanut butter
1/2 cup (125 mL) granulated
    sugar
1/2 cup (125 mL) packed brown
    sugar
1/4 cup (50 mL) butter or
    margarine, softened
1/4 cup (50 mL) vegetable
    shortening
  1 egg
1 1/2 cups (375 mL) all-purpose
    flour
3/4 teaspoon (4 mL) baking soda
1/4 teaspoon (1 mL) salt
3/4 cup (175 mL) miniature
    candy-coated semisweet
    chocolate chips

           4 dozen cookies

Heat oven to 375°F (190°C). In large mixing bowl, combine peanut butter, sugars, butter, shortening and egg. Beat at medium speed of electric mixer until light and fluffy. Add flour, baking soda and salt. Beat at low speed until soft dough forms. Stir in chips.

Shape dough into 1-inch (2.5 cm) balls. Place balls 2 inches (5 cm) apart on un-greased cookie sheets. Flatten balls with fork in crisscross pattern. Bake for 8 to 10 minutes, or until light golden brown. Cool completely before storing.

Snickerdoodles

1 1/2 cups (375 mL) plus
       2 tablespoons (25 mL)
       sugar, divided
  1 cup (250 mL) butter or
       margarine, softened
  2 eggs
2 3/4 cups (675 mL) all-purpose
       flour
  2 teaspoons (10 mL) cream of
       tartar
  1 teaspoon (5 mL) baking soda
 1/2 teaspoon (2 mL) ground
       nutmeg
 1/2 teaspoon (2 mL) salt
  2 tablespoons (25 mL) ground
       cinnamon
 84 pecan halves

                    7 dozen cookies

In large mixing bowl, combine
1 1/2 cups (375 mL) sugar, the
butter and eggs. Beat at medium speed of electric mixer
until light and fluffy. Add
flour, cream of tartar, baking
soda, nutmeg and salt. Beat at
low speed until soft dough
forms. Cover with plastic wrap.
Chill 1 to 2 hours, or until firm.

Heat oven to 375°F (190°C). In
small bowl, combine cinnamon
and remaining 2 tablespoons
(25 mL) sugar. Shape dough
into 1-inch (2.5 cm) balls. Roll
balls in cinnamon mixture. Place
balls 2 inches (5 cm) apart on
ungreased cookie sheets. Press
pecan half into center of each
ball. Bake for 10 to 12 minutes,
or until light golden brown.
Let cool for 1 minute before
removing from cookie sheets.
Cool completely before storing.

Shaped Cookies

Orange Spice Cookies

1 cup (250 mL) granulated sugar
1 cup (250 mL) powdered sugar
1 cup (250 mL) butter or margarine, softened
1 cup (250 mL) vegetable shortening
2 eggs
4 cups (1 L) all-purpose flour
2 teaspoons (10 mL) grated orange peel
1 teaspoon (5 mL) cream of tartar
1 teaspoon (5 mL) baking soda
1/2 teaspoon (2 mL) ground cardamom
1/4 teaspoon (1 mL) ground ginger
1/4 teaspoon (1 mL) salt
Granulated sugar

5 1/2 dozen cookies

In large mixing bowl, combine 1 cup (250 mL) granulated sugar, the powdered sugar, butter, shortening and eggs. Beat at medium speed of electric mixer until light and fluffy. Add flour, peel, cream of tartar, baking soda, cardamom, ginger and salt. Beat at low speed until soft dough forms. Cover with plastic wrap. Chill 1 to 2 hours, or until firm.

Heat oven to 350°F (180°C). Shape dough into 1-inch (2.5 cm) balls. Roll balls in granulated sugar. Place balls 2 inches (5 cm) apart on un-greased cookie sheets. Flatten balls with bottom of drinking glass, wiping glass with damp cloth to prevent sticking. Bake for 12 to 13 minutes, or until light golden brown. Let cool for 1 minute before removing from cookie sheets. Cool completely before storing.

Shaped Cookies

22

Peanut Butter No-bake Cookies

2½ cups (625 mL) powdered
    sugar
2 cups (500 mL) graham
    cracker crumbs
1 cup (250 mL) butter or
    margarine, softened
1 cup (250 mL) flaked coconut
¾ cup (175 mL) finely chopped
    dried apricots
½ cup (125 mL) chunky honey-
    roasted peanut butter
⅓ cup (75 mL) granulated
    sugar
1 teaspoon (5 mL) vanilla
    Granulated sugar

3½ dozen cookies

Line airtight container with
wax paper. Set aside. In large
mixing bowl, combine pow-
dered sugar, crumbs, butter,
coconut, apricots, peanut butter, ⅓ cup (75 mL) granulated
sugar and the vanilla. Stir
until well blended.

Shape dough into 1-inch
(2.5 cm) balls. Roll balls in
granulated sugar. Place
balls in prepared container.
Store in refrigerator.

Oatmeal Peanut Snaps

  1 cup (250 mL) granulated sugar
  1 cup (250 mL) packed brown sugar
  3/4 cup (175 mL) butter or margarine, softened
  2 eggs
2 1/4 cups (550 mL) all-purpose flour
  2 cups (500 mL) crisp oatmeal flakes with raisins
  1 teaspoon (5 mL) baking powder
  1 teaspoon (5 mL) baking soda
  1 cup (250 mL) chopped salted peanuts

5 1/2 dozen cookies

In large mixing bowl, combine sugars and butter. Beat at medium speed of electric mixer until light and fluffy. Add eggs, one at a time, beating after each addition. Add flour, oatmeal flakes, baking powder and baking soda. Beat at low speed until soft dough forms. Stir in peanuts. Cover with plastic wrap. Chill 1 to 2 hours, or until firm.

Heat oven to 375°F (190°C). Shape dough into 1-inch (2.5 cm) balls. Place balls 2 inches (5 cm) apart on ungreased cookie sheets. Bake for 12 to 14 minutes, or until golden brown. Cool completely before storing.

Praline Crunch Cookies

1½ cups (375 mL) sugar
 1 cup (250 mL) butter or margarine, softened
 2 eggs
 1 teaspoon (5 mL) vanilla
 3 cups (750 mL) all-purpose flour
 2 teaspoons (10 mL) cream of tartar
 1 teaspoon (5 mL) baking soda
 ¼ teaspoon (1 mL) salt
 1 cup (250 mL) English toffee bits
 ½ cup (125 mL) chopped pecans

5 dozen cookies

In large mixing bowl, combine sugar, butter, eggs and vanilla. Beat at medium speed of electric mixer until light and fluffy. Add flour, cream of tartar, baking soda and salt. Beat at low speed until soft dough forms. Stir in bits and pecans. Cover with plastic wrap. Chill 1 to 2 hours, or until firm.

Heat oven to 375°F (190°C). Shape dough into 1½-inch (4 cm) balls. Place balls 2 inches (5 cm) apart on ungreased cookie sheets. Bake for 9 to 13 minutes, or until light golden brown. Cool completely before storing.

Shaped Cookies

Chinese Almond Cookies

1 cup (250 mL) butter or
  margarine, softened
2/3 cup (150 mL) powdered
  sugar
1 egg
1 teaspoon (5 mL) grated
  lemon peel
1 teaspoon (5 mL) vanilla
1/2 teaspoon (2 mL) almond
  extract
2 1/3 cups (575 mL) all-purpose
  flour
1/2 teaspoon (2 mL) baking
  powder
1 egg yolk beaten with 1
  tablespoon (15 mL) water
24 whole blanched almonds

            3 dozen cookies

Heat oven to 350°F (180°C). In
large mixing bowl, combine
butter, sugar, egg, peel, vanilla
and almond extract. Beat at
medium speed of electric
mixer until light and fluffy.
Add flour and baking powder.
Beat at low speed until soft
dough forms.

Shape dough into 1-inch
(2.5 cm) balls. Place balls
2 inches (5 cm) apart on ungreased cookie sheets. Flatten
balls with bottom of drinking
glass, wiping glass with damp
cloth to prevent sticking.

Lightly brush tops of cookies
with egg yolk mixture. Press
almond into center of each
cookie. Bake for 13 to 15 minutes, or until edges are light
golden brown. Cool completely before storing.

Crinkled Molasses Cookies

    1   cup (250 mL) sugar
   3/4 cup (175 mL) vegetable
        shortening
   1/4 cup (50 mL) light molasses
    1   egg
    2   cups (500 mL) all-purpose
        flour
  2 1/2 teaspoons (12 mL) baking
        soda
    1   teaspoon (5 mL) ground
        cinnamon
    1   teaspoon (5 mL) ground
        ginger
   1/2 teaspoon (2 mL) ground
        cloves
   1/4 teaspoon (1 mL) ground
        cardamom
   1/4 teaspoon (1 mL) salt
        Granulated sugar

                    6 dozen cookies

Heat oven to 350°F (180°C). In large mixing bowl, combine 1 cup (250 mL) sugar, the shortening, molasses and egg. Beat at medium speed of electric mixer until well blended. Add flour, baking soda, cinnamon, ginger, cloves, cardamom and salt. Beat at low speed until soft dough forms.

Shape dough into 1-inch (2.5 cm) balls. Roll balls in granulated sugar. Place balls 2 inches (5 cm) apart on ungreased cookie sheets. Bake for 8 to 12 minutes, or until set. Cool completely before storing.

Orange Mocha Crinkles

2 cups (500 mL) granulated
  sugar
½ cup (125 mL) vegetable oil
4 squares (1 oz./30 g each)
  unsweetened baking
  chocolate, melted
½ teaspoon (2 mL) grated
  orange peel
½ teaspoon (2 mL) orange
  extract
1 tablespoon (15 mL) instant
  coffee crystals
1 tablespoon (15 mL) hot water
4 eggs
3 cups (750 mL) all-purpose
  flour
2 teaspoons (10 mL) baking
  powder
¼ teaspoon (1 mL) salt
  Powdered sugar

           9 dozen cookies

In large mixing bowl, combine granulated sugar, oil, melted chocolate, peel and orange extract. Beat at medium speed of electric mixer until well blended. Set aside.

In small bowl, combine coffee crystals and water. Stir until crystals are dissolved. Add coffee to sugar mixture. Beat at medium speed until well blended. Add eggs, one at a time, beating after each addition. Add flour, baking powder and salt. Beat at low speed until soft dough forms. Cover with plastic wrap. Refrigerate overnight.

Heat oven to 350°F (180°C). Shape dough into 1-inch (2.5 cm) balls. Roll balls in powdered sugar. Place balls 2 inches (5 cm) apart on ungreased cookie sheets. Bake for 12 to 15 minutes, or until set. Cool completely before storing.

Chocolate Mocha Crescents

2 cups (500 mL) sugar
1/2 cup (125 mL) vegetable oil
4 squares (1 oz./30 g each)
    unsweetened baking
    chocolate, melted
2 teaspoons (10 mL) instant
    coffee crystals
2 teaspoons (10 mL) hot water
1 teaspoon (5 mL) vanilla
4 eggs
3 cups (750 mL) all-purpose
    flour
2 teaspoons (10 mL) baking
    powder
1/4 teaspoon (1 mL) salt

Glazes:

1/2 cup (125 mL) semisweet
    chocolate chips
4 teaspoons (20 mL) vegetable
    shortening, divided
1/2 cup (125 mL) vanilla baking
    chips

5 dozen cookies

In large mixing bowl, combine sugar, oil, melted chocolate, coffee crystals, water and vanilla. Beat at medium speed of electric mixer until well blended. Add eggs, one at a time, beating after each addition. Add flour, baking powder and salt. Beat at low speed until soft dough forms. Cover with plastic wrap. Chill 3 to 4 hours, or until firm.

Heat oven to 350°F (180°C). Shape rounded measuring tablespoons (15 mL) dough into crescent shapes. Place crescents 2 inches (5 cm) apart on ungreased cookie sheets. Bake for 12 to 15 minutes, or until set. Cool completely.

In 1-quart (1 L) saucepan, combine chocolate chips and 2 teaspoons (10 mL) shortening. Melt over low heat, stirring constantly. Set glaze aside. Repeat with vanilla chips and remaining 2 teaspoons (10 mL) shortening. Drizzle small amount of chocolate glaze over each cookie. Repeat with vanilla glaze. Let dry completely before storing.

Microwave tip: In small bowl, combine chocolate chips and 2 teaspoons (10 mL) shortening. In second small bowl, combine vanilla chips and remaining 2 teaspoons (10 mL) shortening. Place bowls in microwave. Melt chips at 50% (Medium) for 3 1/2 to 4 minutes, stirring chip mixtures after every minute. (Vanilla chips may melt before chocolate chips. If so, remove from oven and continue microwaving chocolate chips.) Continue as directed.

Shaped Cookies

Peppermint Bon Bons

1 cup (250 mL) granulated
    sugar
1/2 cup (125 mL) butter or
    margarine, softened
1/2 cup (125 mL) vegetable
    shortening
1/2 cup (125 mL) unsweetened
    cocoa
1/2 cup (125 mL) buttermilk
2 eggs
1/4 teaspoon (1 mL) peppermint
    extract
3 cups (750 mL) all-purpose
    flour
1/2 teaspoon (2 mL) baking soda
1/4 teaspoon (1 mL) salt

Frosting:
2 cups (500 mL) powdered
    sugar
2 to 4 tablespoons (25 to
    50 mL) whipping cream
2 tablespoons (25 mL) butter
    or margarine, softened
1 or 2 drops green food
    coloring

5 dozen cookies

In large mixing bowl, combine granulated sugar, 1/2 cup (125 mL) butter, the shortening, cocoa, buttermilk, eggs and peppermint extract. Beat at medium speed of electric mixer until well blended. Add flour, baking soda and salt. Beat at low speed until soft dough forms. Cover with plastic wrap. Chill 3 to 4 hours, or until firm.

Heat oven to 350°F (180°C). Shape dough into 1-inch (2.5 cm) balls. Place balls 2 inches (5 cm) apart on ungreased cookie sheets. Bake for 10 to 14 minutes, or until set. Cool completely.

In medium mixing bowl, combine frosting ingredients. Beat at low speed of electric mixer until smooth. Spread frosting evenly on cookies. Let dry completely before storing.

Peanut Butter 'n Jelly Thumbprints

3/4 cup (175 mL) chunky honey-roasted peanut butter, divided
1/2 cup (125 mL) granulated sugar
1/2 cup (125 mL) packed brown sugar
1/2 cup (125 mL) butter or margarine, softened
1 egg
1 1/4 cups (300 mL) all-purpose flour
3/4 teaspoon (4 mL) baking soda
1/2 teaspoon (2 mL) baking powder
1/4 teaspoon (1 mL) salt
1/4 cup (50 mL) jam or jelly (any flavor)

3 1/2 dozen cookies

In large mixing bowl, combine 1/2 cup (125 mL) peanut butter, the sugars, butter and egg. Beat at medium speed of electric mixer until light and fluffy. Add flour, baking soda, baking powder and salt. Beat at low speed until soft dough forms. Cover with plastic wrap. Chill 3 to 4 hours, or until firm.

Heat oven to 375°F (190°C). Shape dough into 1-inch (2.5 cm) balls. Place balls 2 inches (5 cm) apart on ungreased cookie sheets. Indent top of each cookie with thumb. Bake for 12 to 15 minutes, or until set.

Immediately indent cookies again. Spoon 1/4 teaspoon (1 mL) each of jelly and remaining peanut butter into each thumbprint. Cool completely before storing. (Do not stack cookies.)

Tip: Use end of spoon to make indentation in hot cookies.

Rolled Cookie Basics

Rolled, or cutout, cookies are made by rolling out firm dough and then cutting it into shapes with cookie cutters. Simple shapes like circles or squares can be cut with a sharp knife, or the rim of a glass dipped in sugar or flour can be used as a cutter.

The thinner the dough is rolled, the crisper the resulting cookies will be. Follow individual recipes for dough thickness.

Cookie cutters are available in a wide variety of shapes and sizes. Purchase them almost anywhere that cooking equipment is sold, or design your own, as shown below.

How to Design Your Own Cutout Cookies

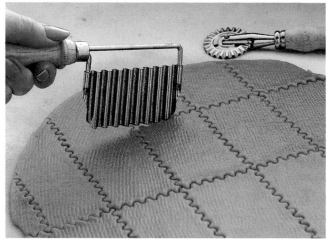

Pick a design you like, and trace it onto heavy cardboard. Cut out the design, and use it as a pattern on rolled-out cookie dough. Cut around the pattern with a sharp knife.

Use a crinkle cutter or a pastry wheel to make cookies with patterned edges.

How to Make Rolled Cookies — 3 Basic Steps

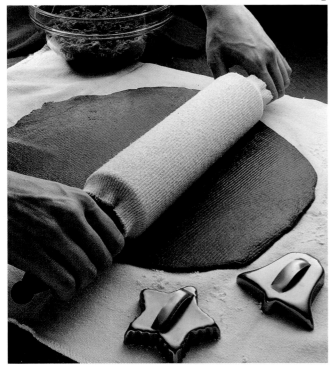

1) Work with small amounts of dough at a time when rolling it out. (Refrigerate remaining dough until you are ready to use it.) Lightly dust the countertop with flour or cover it with a floured pastry cloth to keep dough from sticking. A rolling pin cover, or stockinette, also minimizes sticking.

2) Cut shapes in dough as close together as possible, dipping cookie cutters in sugar or flour occasionally to keep cutters from sticking. Gently remove and press dough scraps together for rerolling. (Too much handling of dough can result in tough cookies, however.)

3) Use a wide spatula to transfer cutout shapes from countertop to cookie sheets, and to remove baked cookies from sheets and transfer them to cooling racks.

Rolled Cookies

Apricot Stars (top)

> 1 cup (250 mL) sugar
> 1 cup (250 mL) butter or margarine, softened
> 1 egg
> 1 teaspoon (5 mL) almond extract
> 3¼ cups (800 mL) all-purpose flour
> ½ cup (125 mL) ground almonds
> 1 teaspoon (5 mL) baking powder
> ¼ teaspoon (1 mL) salt
> ½ cup (125 mL) apricot preserves or other tart
>   preserves

About 3 dozen cookies

In large mixing bowl, combine sugar, butter, egg and almond extract. Beat at medium speed of electric mixer until light and fluffy. Add flour, almonds, baking powder and salt. Beat at low speed until soft dough forms. Cover with plastic wrap. Chill 2 to 3 hours, or until firm.

Heat oven to 400°F (200°C). On floured surface, roll dough to ¼-inch (5 mm) thickness. Using 3½ and 2-inch (9 and 5 cm) star cookie cutters, cut shapes into dough. (Cut equal number of each size star.) Using 1-inch (2.5 cm) round cookie cutter, cut center out of small stars.

Place large stars 2 inches (5 cm) apart on ungreased cookie sheets. Place small stars on top of large stars. Spoon heaping ¼ teaspoon (1 mL) preserves into center of each small star. Bake for 8 to 10 minutes, or until edges are light golden brown. Cool completely before storing.

Peanut Butter Dinosaurs (bottom)

> ¾ cup (175 mL) butter or margarine, softened
> ¾ cup (175 mL) creamy peanut butter
> ½ cup (125 mL) granulated sugar
> ½ cup (125 mL) packed brown sugar
> 1 egg
> 1 teaspoon (5 mL) vanilla
> 2½ cups (625 mL) all-purpose flour
> ½ teaspoon (2 mL) salt
>   Decorator Frosting (see page 246)

About 3 dozen cookies

In large mixing bowl, combine butter, peanut butter, sugars, egg and vanilla. Beat at medium speed of electric mixer until light and fluffy. Add flour and salt. Beat at low speed until soft dough forms.

Divide dough in half. Cover with plastic wrap. Chill 2 to 3 hours, or until firm.

Heat oven to 350°F (180°C). On well-floured surface, roll half of dough to ¼-inch (5 mm) thickness (dough will be fragile). Using 4 to 5-inch (10 to 12 cm) dinosaur cookie cutters, cut shapes into dough.

Place shapes 2 inches (5 cm) apart on ungreased cookie sheets. Repeat with remaining dough. Bake for 10 to 13 minutes, or until set. Cool completely. Prepare frosting as directed. Decorate cookies as desired. Let dry completely before storing.

Butterscotch Tea Party Cookies

1   cup (250 mL) butter or
    margarine, softened
2/3 cup (150 mL) packed brown
    sugar
1/3 cup (75 mL) granulated
    sugar
1   egg
2   teaspoons (10 mL) vanilla
3   cups (750 mL) all-purpose
    flour
1   cup (250 mL) butterscotch
    chips, melted
2   tablespoons (25 mL) milk
1/2 teaspoon (2 mL) baking soda

About 6 dozen cookies

In large mixing bowl, combine butter, sugars, egg and vanilla. Beat at medium speed of electric mixer until light and fluffy. Add flour, melted chips, milk and baking soda. Beat at low speed until soft dough forms. Cover with plastic wrap. Chill 3 to 4 hours, or until firm.

Heat oven to 350°F (180°C). Divide dough into thirds. Cover 2/3 dough with plastic wrap. Chill. On lightly floured surface, roll remaining third dough to 1/4-inch (5 mm) thickness. Using 2 to 3-inch (5 to 8 cm) cookie cutters, cut desired shapes into dough.

Place shapes 2 inches (5 cm) apart on ungreased cookie sheets. Repeat with remaining dough. Bake for 6 to 7 minutes, or until edges are golden brown. Cool completely. If desired, decorate cookies with favorite frosting. Let dry completely before storing.

Tip: If desired, sprinkle cookies with additional granulated sugar before baking.

Card Party Cookies

Filling:

- 1 cup (250 mL) chopped dates
- 3/4 cup (175 mL) dried cranberries
- 1/4 cup (50 mL) granulated sugar
- 2 tablespoons (25 mL) water

- 1 cup (250 mL) butter or margarine, softened
- 1/2 cup (125 mL) packed brown sugar
- 1/4 cup (50 mL) granulated sugar
- 1 egg
- 3 cups (750 mL) all-purpose flour
- 1/4 teaspoon (1 mL) baking powder
- 1/4 teaspoon (1 mL) salt

About 2½ dozen cookies

In 2-quart (2 L) saucepan, combine filling ingredients. Cook over medium heat until slightly thickened, stirring constantly. Set aside. Heat oven to 350°F (180°C). In large mixing bowl, combine butter, sugars and egg. Beat at medium speed of electric mixer until light and fluffy. Add flour, baking powder and salt. Beat at low speed until soft dough forms.

Divide dough in half. On well-floured surface, roll half of dough to 1/4-inch (5 mm) thickness. Using 3-inch (8 cm) round cookie cutter, cut circles into dough. Using 1-inch (2.5 cm) shaped cookie cutters (heart, diamond, spade, club) cut out center of half of circles. Set small shapes aside.

Place whole circles 2 inches (5 cm) apart on ungreased cookie sheets. Spoon 1 teaspoon (5 mL) filling onto center of each. Top with cut circles, pressing with fork to seal edges. Place small shapes on tops of cookies. Repeat with remaining dough. Bake for 11 to 13 minutes, or until edges are light golden brown. Cool completely before storing.

Rolled Cookies

Chocolate Heart Party Bears

    1   cup (250 mL) granulated sugar
    1   cup (250 mL) butter or margarine, softened
    1   pkg. (3 oz./85 g) cream cheese, softened
    1   egg
    1   teaspoon (5 mL) vanilla
    ½   teaspoon (2 mL) chocolate extract
    3   cups (750 mL) all-purpose flour
    ½   cup (125 mL) unsweetened cocoa
        Rainbow semisweet chocolate chips
        Miniature candy-coated semisweet chocolate
          chips

Frosting:
    2   cups (500 mL) powdered sugar
    2   to 3 tablespoons (25 to 50 mL) half-and-half
    2   tablespoons (25 mL) butter or margarine,
          softened
    1   or 2 drops red food coloring

                                    5 dozen cookies

In large mixing bowl, combine granulated sugar, 1 cup (250 mL) butter, the cream cheese, egg, vanilla and chocolate extract. Beat at medium speed of electric mixer until light and fluffy. Add flour and cocoa. Beat at low speed until soft dough forms. Divide dough in half. Cover with plastic wrap. Chill 1 to 2 hours, or until firm.

Heat oven to 350°F (180°C). On well-floured surface, roll half of dough to ¼-inch (5 mm) thickness. Using 3-inch (8 cm) teddy bear cookie cutter and 1-inch (2.5 cm) heart cookie cutter, cut shapes into dough. (Cut equal number of bears and hearts.)

Place bear shapes 2 inches (5 cm) apart on ungreased cookie sheets. Place 1 heart on paw of each bear. Repeat with remaining dough. Decorate each bear with rainbow chip for belly button and miniature chips for eyes. Bake for 8 to 10 minutes, or until set. Cool completely.

In small mixing bowl, combine frosting ingredients. Using pastry bag with #2 writing tip, pipe outline on hearts, paws and ears. Pipe on mouth. Let dry completely before storing.

Choco-Mint Pillows

1 cup (250 mL) sugar
1 cup (250 mL) butter or
   margarine, softened
1 egg
1 teaspoon (5 mL) vanilla
3 cups (750 mL) all-purpose
   flour
1 teaspoon (5 mL) baking
   powder
1/4 teaspoon (1 mL) salt
49 chocolate sandwich mints

   About 4 dozen cookies

Heat oven to 400°F (200°C). In large mixing bowl, combine sugar, butter, egg and vanilla. Beat at medium speed of electric mixer until light and fluffy. Add flour, baking powder and salt. Beat at low speed until soft dough forms.

Divide dough in half. On well-floured surface, roll half of dough into 13 x 9-inch (33 x 23 cm) rectangle. Arrange mints evenly on dough, forming 7 rows of 7. Between 2 sheets of wax paper, roll remaining dough into 13 x 9-inch (33 x 23 cm) rectangle.

Discard top sheet of wax paper. Carefully turn second rectangle over mint-topped dough, matching edges. Using scalloped pastry wheel, cut dough evenly between mints. Gently press edges of pillows to seal.

Place pillows 2 inches (5 cm) apart on ungreased cookie sheets. Bake for 9 to 12 minutes, or until edges are light golden brown. Cool completely before storing.

Nutmeg Squares

½ cup (125 mL) sugar
½ cup (125 mL) butter or
 margarine, softened
1 egg
1 tablespoon (15 mL)
 whipping cream
1 teaspoon (5 mL) vanilla
2 cups (500 mL) all-purpose
 flour
1 teaspoon (5 mL) baking
 powder
½ teaspoon (2 mL) baking soda
½ teaspoon (2 mL) ground
 nutmeg
½ cup (125 mL) semisweet
 chocolate chips
2 teaspoons (10 mL) vegetable
 shortening, divided
½ cup (125 mL) vanilla baking
 chips
½ cup (125 mL) coarsely
 chopped pistachios

  About 3 dozen cookies

Heat oven to 350°F (180°C). In large mixing bowl, combine sugar, butter, egg, cream and vanilla. Beat at medium speed of electric mixer until well blended. Add flour, baking powder, baking soda and nutmeg. Beat at low speed until soft dough forms. Cover with plastic wrap. Chill 3 to 4 hours, or until firm.

On lightly floured surface, roll dough to ⅛ to ¼-inch (3 to 5 mm) thickness. Using 3-inch (8 cm) square cookie cutter, cut squares into dough. Place squares 2 inches (5 cm) apart on ungreased cookie sheets. Bake for 8 to 10 minutes, or until edges are golden brown. Cool completely.

In 1-quart (1 L) saucepan, combine chocolate chips and 1 teaspoon (5 mL) shortening. Melt over low heat, stirring constantly. Set aside. Repeat with vanilla chips and remaining 1 teaspoon (5 mL) shortening. (If desired, transfer melted chips to custard cups.)

Dip one corner of each cookie into melted chocolate chips. Sprinkle pistachios evenly over dipped corners. Repeat with opposite corner in melted vanilla chips and remaining pistachios. Let dry completely before storing.

Rolled Cookies

Brown Sugar Cookies

- 1 cup (250 mL) butter or margarine, softened
- 1/2 cup (125 mL) packed brown sugar
- 1/4 cup (50 mL) granulated sugar
- 1 teaspoon (5 mL) vanilla
- 2 1/4 cups (550 mL) all-purpose flour
- 1/2 teaspoon (2 mL) salt

Frosting:

- 3/4 cup (175 mL) packed brown sugar
- 1/4 cup (50 mL) butter or margarine
- 1 1/4 cups (300 mL) powdered sugar
- 1 to 2 tablespoons (15 to 25 mL) half-and-half
- 1 teaspoon (5 mL) vanilla

About 6 dozen cookies

Heat oven to 300°F (150°C). In large mixing bowl, combine 1 cup (250 mL) butter, 1/2 cup (125 mL) brown sugar, the granulated sugar and 1 teaspoon (5 mL) vanilla. Beat at medium speed of electric mixer until light and fluffy. Add flour and salt. Beat at low speed until soft dough forms. Form dough into ball.

On well-floured surface, roll dough to 1/4 to 1/2-inch (5 mm to 1 cm) thickness. Using 2-inch (5 cm) round cookie cutter, cut circles into dough. Place circles 2 inches (5 cm) apart on ungreased cookie sheets. Bake for 20 to 25 minutes, or until golden brown. Cool completely.

In 1-quart (1 L) saucepan, combine 3/4 cup (175 mL) brown sugar and 1/4 cup (50 mL) butter. Cook over medium heat until butter is melted, stirring constantly. Remove from heat. Add remaining frosting ingredients. Stir until smooth. Spread frosting evenly on cookies. Let dry completely before storing.

Rolled Cookies

Refrigerated Cookie Basics

Refrigerated cookies, sometimes called slice-and-bake cookies, are perfect when time is limited. The dough can be made ahead of time and refrigerated until you are ready to bake. After the dough is mixed, it is usually rolled into a log; the log can be rolled in chopped nuts or other coatings and then wrapped tightly with plastic wrap or wax paper. The prepared dough is then chilled until it is firm enough to slice. Dough can usually be stored in the coldest part of the

How to Make Refrigerated Cookies — 4 Basic Steps

1) Shape dough into log, with hands, on lightly floured surface or lightly floured wax paper.

2) Roll the log in chopped nuts, coconut, colored shot or other coatings, on wax paper or in shallow dish, as called for in certain recipes.

refrigerator for up to one week, or it can be frozen for longer storage. To freeze dough, overwrap the plastic wrap with foil or place the dough in resealable freezer bags. To thaw frozen cookie dough, move it from the freezer to the refrigerator one to two hours before you plan to slice and bake. Because these cookies are thinly sliced, solid ingredients such as nuts or dried fruit need to be finely chopped so the dough can be easily sliced without tearing.

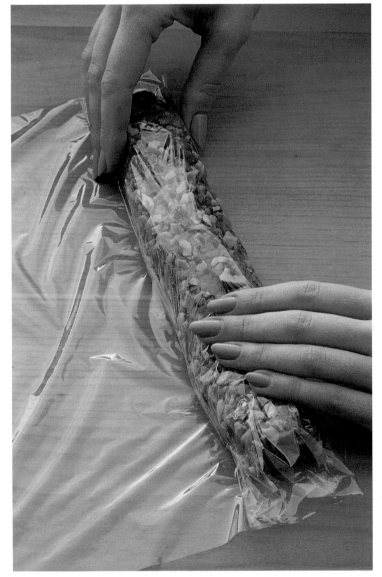

3) Wrap log tightly in plastic wrap or wax paper. Refrigerate until log is firm enough to slice.

4) Remove the wrap from the log when ready to bake the cookies, and slice crosswise, using a serrated or thin-bladed knife. Rotate the log as you slice to avoid flattening one side. Make sure slices of dough have a uniform thickness so the cookies will bake evenly and in the same amount of time.

Refrigerated Cookies

Whole Wheat Peanut Butter Slices

1/2 cup (125 mL) granulated sugar
1/2 cup (125 mL) packed brown sugar
1/2 cup (125 mL) butter or margarine,
  softened
1/3 cup (75 mL) creamy honey-roasted peanut
  butter
1 egg
1 teaspoon (5 mL) vanilla
13/4 cups (425 mL) whole wheat flour
1/4 cup (50 mL) all-purpose flour
1 teaspoon (5 mL) baking powder
1/2 teaspoon (2 mL) baking soda
1/4 teaspoon (1 mL) salt
1/2 cup (125 mL) finely chopped honey-roasted
  peanuts

5 dozen cookies

In large mixing bowl, combine sugars, butter, peanut butter, egg and vanilla. Beat at medium speed of electric mixer until light and fluffy. Add flours, baking powder, baking soda and salt. Beat at low speed until soft dough forms.

Divide dough in half. On lightly floured wax paper, shape each half into 13/4-inch-diameter (4.5 cm) log. Roll logs evenly in peanuts, pressing lightly to coat. Wrap in plastic wrap or wax paper. Chill 3 to 4 hours, or until firm.

Heat oven to 375°F (190°C). Cut logs into 1/4-inch (5 mm) slices. Place slices 2 inches (5 cm) apart on ungreased cookie sheets. Bake for 6 to 8 minutes, or until set. Cool completely before storing.

Refrigerated Cookies

Orange Ginger Cookies

2 cups (500 mL) granulated sugar
1 cup (250 mL) vegetable shortening
1/2 cup (125 mL) butter or margarine, softened
1/2 cup (125 mL) light molasses
2 eggs
4 cups (1 L) all-purpose flour
2 teaspoons (10 mL) baking soda
2 teaspoons (10 mL) ground cinnamon
2 teaspoons (10 mL) ground ginger
2 teaspoons (10 mL) ground allspice
2 teaspoons (10 mL) grated orange peel
1/4 teaspoon (1 mL) salt
  Granulated sugar

8 1/2 dozen cookies

In large mixing bowl, combine 2 cups (500 mL) sugar, the shortening, butter, molasses and eggs. Beat at medium speed of electric mixer until light and fluffy. Add flour, baking soda, cinnamon, ginger, allspice, peel and salt. Beat at low speed until soft dough forms.

Divide dough into quarters. Shape each quarter into 2-inch-diameter (5 cm) log. Wrap in plastic wrap or wax paper. Refrigerate overnight.

Heat oven to 350°F (180°C). Cut logs into 1/4-inch (5 mm) slices. Place slices 2 inches (5 cm) apart on ungreased cookie sheets. Bake for 9 to 12 minutes, or until set. Immediately sprinkle with granulated sugar. Cool completely before storing.

Cran-Raspberry Pinwheels

Filling:

1 *pkg. (10 oz./283.8 g) frozen raspberries in juice, defrosted*
½ *cup (125 mL) dried cranberries*
2 *tablespoons (25 mL) cornstarch*
1 *tablespoon (15 mL) lemon juice*

¾ *cup (175 mL) packed brown sugar*
½ *cup (125 mL) butter or margarine, softened*
1 *egg*
½ *teaspoon (2 mL) vanilla*
2 *cups (500 mL) all-purpose flour*
1 *teaspoon (5 mL) grated lemon peel*
½ *teaspoon (2 mL) baking soda*
¼ *teaspoon (1 mL) salt*

4½ dozen cookies

In 1-quart (1 L) saucepan, combine filling ingredients. Cook over medium heat for 5 to 7 minutes, or until thickened, stirring constantly. Cool completely. Set aside.

In large mixing bowl, combine sugar, butter, egg and vanilla. Beat at medium speed of electric mixer until light and fluffy. Add flour, peel, baking soda and salt. Beat at low speed until soft dough forms.

On well-floured surface, roll dough into 12 x 8-inch (30 x 20 cm) rectangle. Spread filling to within 1 inch (2.5 cm) of edges. Roll dough, jelly roll style, starting with long side. Pinch edge to seal. Cut roll in half crosswise. Wrap in plastic wrap or wax paper. Refrigerate overnight.

Heat oven to 375°F (190°C). Lightly grease cookie sheets. Cut rolls into ½-inch (1 cm) slices. Place slices 2 inches (5 cm) apart on prepared cookie sheets. Bake for 9 to 13 minutes, or until edges are light golden brown. Cool completely before storing.

Maple Walnut Refrigerator Cookies

2 cups (500 mL) packed brown
   sugar
1 cup (250 mL) butter or
   margarine, softened
3 eggs
1/2 teaspoon (2 mL) maple
   extract
2 1/2 cups (625 mL) all-purpose
   flour
1 cup (250 mL) whole wheat
   flour
1 cup (250 mL) finely chopped
   walnuts
1 teaspoon (5 mL) baking soda
   Pinch of salt

2 1/2 dozen cookies

In large mixing bowl, combine sugar, butter, eggs and maple extract. Beat at medium speed of electric mixer until light and fluffy. Add flours, walnuts, baking soda and salt. Beat at low speed until soft dough forms.

Line 8 x 4-inch (1.5 L) loaf pan with wax paper. Press dough evenly into prepared pan. Cover with plastic wrap. Chill 3 to 4 hours, or until firm.

Heat oven to 350°F (180°C). Remove dough from pan. Discard wax paper. Cut dough in half lengthwise. Cut halves crosswise into 1/4-inch (5 mm) slices. Place slices 2 inches (5 cm) apart on ungreased cookie sheets. Bake for 8 to 10 minutes, or until edges are golden brown. Cool completely before storing.

Lemon Lover Cookies

3/4 cup (175 mL) butter or margarine, softened
3 tablespoons (50 mL) granulated sugar
1¼ cups (300 mL) all-purpose flour
½ cup (125 mL) cornstarch
1 teaspoon (5 mL) grated lemon peel
2 tablespoons (25 mL) fresh lemon juice

Frosting:
1 cup (250 mL) powdered sugar
¼ cup (50 mL) butter or margarine, softened
1 teaspoon (5 mL) grated lemon peel
1 to 2 teaspoons (5 to 10 mL) fresh lemon juice

3½ dozen cookies

In large mixing bowl, combine 3/4 cup (175 mL) butter and the granulated sugar. Beat at medium speed of electric mixer until light and fluffy. Add flour, cornstarch, 1 teaspoon (5 mL) peel and 2 tablespoons (25 mL) juice. Beat at low speed until soft dough forms. Shape dough into 1½-inch-diameter (4 cm) log. Wrap in plastic wrap or wax paper. Chill 1 to 2 hours, or until firm.

Heat oven to 350°F (180°C). Cut log into ¼-inch (5 mm) slices. Place slices 2 inches (5 cm) apart on ungreased cookie sheets. Bake for 8 to 10 minutes, or until edges are light golden brown. Cool completely. In small mixing bowl, combine frosting ingredients. Beat at medium speed of electric mixer until smooth. Spread frosting evenly on cookies. Let dry completely before storing.

Refrigerated Cookies

Chocolate Chip Sunflower Cookies

1 cup (250 mL) sugar
3/4 cup (175 mL) butter or
   margarine, softened
1/2 cup (125 mL) vegetable
   shortening
1/2 teaspoon (2 mL) vanilla
2 1/4 cups (550 mL) all-purpose
   flour
1/2 teaspoon (2 mL) baking soda
1/2 cup (125 mL) miniature
   semisweet chocolate chips
1/2 cup (125 mL) shelled
   sunflower seeds
1/2 cup (125 mL) flaked coconut

About 3 1/2 dozen cookies

In large mixing bowl, combine sugar, butter, shortening and vanilla. Beat at medium speed of electric mixer until light and fluffy. Add flour and baking soda. Beat at low speed until soft dough forms. Stir in chips and seeds. Divide dough in half. Shape each half into 2-inch-diameter (5 cm) log. Roll logs evenly in coconut, pressing lightly to coat. Wrap in plastic wrap or wax paper. Chill 2 to 3 hours, or until firm.

Heat oven to 350°F (180°C). Cut logs into 1/4 to 1/2-inch (5 mm to 1 cm) slices. Place slices 2 inches (5 cm) apart on ungreased cookie sheets. Bake for 13 to 15 minutes, or until set and edges are golden brown. Let cool for 1 minute before removing from cookie sheets. Cool completely before storing.

Coffee Spice Cookies

  1 teaspoon (5 mL) instant
    coffee crystals
  1 teaspoon (5 mL) hot water
  3/4 cup (175 mL) packed brown
    sugar
  1/2 cup (125 mL) butter or
    margarine, softened
  1 egg
  1/2 teaspoon (2 mL) vanilla
  1 1/2 cups (375 mL) all-purpose
    flour
  1 teaspoon (5 mL) baking
    powder
  1/2 teaspoon (2 mL) ground
    allspice
  1/4 teaspoon (1 mL) salt
  1/3 cup (75 mL) candy sprinkles
    or multicolored shot

About 5 1/2 dozen cookies

In small bowl, combine coffee crystals and water. Stir until crystals are dissolved. In large mixing bowl, combine coffee, sugar, butter, egg and vanilla. Beat at medium speed of electric mixer until light and fluffy. Add flour, baking powder, allspice and salt. Beat at low speed until soft dough forms. Divide dough in half. Shape each half into 1 1/2-inch-diameter (4 cm) log.

Roll logs evenly in sprinkles, pressing lightly to coat. Wrap in plastic wrap or wax paper. Chill 3 to 4 hours, or until firm. Heat oven to 375°F (190°C). Cut logs into 1/4-inch (5 mm) slices. Place slices 2 inches (5 cm) apart on ungreased cookie sheets. Bake for 6 to 8 minutes, or until set. Cool completely before storing.

Refrigerated Cookies

Date Pinwheel Cookies

Filling:

  1 *cup (250 mL) chopped dates*
  1/3 *cup (75 mL) orange juice*
  1/4 *cup (50 mL) granulated sugar*
  1/2 *teaspoon (2 mL) vanilla*

  1 *cup (250 mL) packed brown sugar*
  1/2 *cup (125 mL) butter or margarine, softened*
  1 *egg*
1 3/4 *cups (425 mL) all-purpose flour*
  2 *teaspoons (10 mL) grated orange peel*
1 1/2 *teaspoons (7 mL) baking powder*
  1/4 *teaspoon (1 mL) salt*

4 1/2 dozen cookies

In 1-quart (1 L) saucepan, combine filling ingredients. Cook over medium heat for 5 to 7 minutes, or until thickened, stirring constantly. Cool completely. Set filling aside.

In large mixing bowl, combine brown sugar, butter and egg. Beat at medium speed of electric mixer until light and fluffy. Add flour, peel, baking powder and salt. Beat at low speed until soft dough forms. Cover with plastic wrap. Chill 1 to 2 hours, or until firm.

On floured surface, roll dough into 16 x 8-inch (40 x 20 cm) rectangle. Spread filling to within 1/4 inch (5 mm) of edges. Roll dough, jelly roll style, starting with long side. Pinch edge to seal. Cut roll in half crosswise. Wrap in plastic wrap or wax paper. Chill 2 to 3 hours, or until firm. Heat oven to 375°F (190°C). Cut rolls into 1/4-inch (5 mm) slices. Place slices 2 inches (5 cm) apart on ungreased cookie sheets. Bake for 6 to 9 minutes, or until light golden brown. Cool completely before storing.

Refrigerated Cookies

51

Pinstripe Cookies (left)

1 cup (250 mL) sugar
1 cup (250 mL) butter or margarine, softened
1 egg
1 teaspoon (5 mL) vanilla
2¹/2 cups (625 mL) plus 1 tablespoon (15 mL)
   all-purpose flour, divided
1¹/2 teaspoons (7 mL) baking powder
¹/2 teaspoon (2 mL) salt
1 tablespoon (15 mL) poppy seed
¹/2 teaspoon (2 mL) almond extract
¹/3 cup (75 mL) chopped maraschino cherries,
   well drained
¹/4 teaspoon (1 mL) cherry extract
2 drops red food coloring
3 tablespoons (50 mL) unsweetened cocoa

5¹/2 dozen cookies

Line 9 x 5-inch (2 L) loaf pan with wax paper. Set aside. In large mixing bowl, combine sugar, butter, egg and vanilla. Beat at medium speed of electric mixer until light and fluffy. Add 2¹/2 cups (625 mL) flour, the baking powder and salt. Beat at low speed until soft dough forms.

Divide dough into thirds. Stir poppy seed and almond extract into one third. Press poppy seed mixture evenly into bottom of prepared pan. Stir cherries, remaining 1 tablespoon (15 mL) flour, the cherry extract and food coloring into second third. Press cherry mixture evenly over poppy seed layer. Stir cocoa into remaining third. Press cocoa mixture evenly over cherry layer. Cover with plastic wrap. Refrigerate overnight. Heat oven to 350°F (180°C). Remove dough from pan. Discard wax paper.

Slice dough in half lengthwise. Cut halves crosswise into ¹/8-inch (3 mm) slices. Place slices 2 inches (5 cm) apart on ungreased cookie sheets. Bake for 4 to 6 minutes, or until set. Cool completely before storing.

Mint Chocolate Pinwheels (right)

²/3 cup (150 mL) sugar
¹/2 cup (125 mL) butter or margarine, softened
1 egg
1 tablespoon (15 mL) milk
1 teaspoon (5 mL) vanilla
2 cups (500 mL) all-purpose flour
1 teaspoon (5 mL) baking powder
¹/2 teaspoon (2 mL) salt
¹/3 cup (75 mL) mint chocolate chips, melted and
   slightly cooled

4 dozen cookies

In large mixing bowl, combine sugar, butter, egg, milk and vanilla. Beat at medium speed of electric mixer until light and fluffy. Add flour, baking powder and salt. Beat at low speed until soft dough forms. Divide dough in half. In large mixing bowl, combine half of dough and the melted chips. Beat at low speed until well blended. On lightly floured wax paper, roll chocolate dough into ¹/8-inch-thick (3 mm) rectangle. On second sheet of lightly floured wax paper, roll remaining dough into ¹/8-inch-thick (3 mm) rectangle.

Turn white rectangle carefully onto chocolate rectangle, matching edges. Discard top sheet of wax paper. Roll dough, jelly roll style, starting with long side. (Peel off wax paper when rolling.) Pinch edge to seal. Wrap in plastic wrap or wax paper. Chill 2 to 3 hours, or until firm.

Heat oven to 350°F (180°C). Cut roll into ¹/4-inch (5 mm) slices. Place slices 2 inches (5 cm) apart on ungreased cookie sheets. Bake for 8 to 10 minutes, or until set. Cool completely before storing.

Pecan Crisps

2½ cups (625 mL) packed brown sugar
½ cup (125 mL) butter or margarine, softened
½ cup (125 mL) vegetable shortening
2 eggs
½ teaspoon (2 mL) vanilla
3 cups (750 mL) all-purpose flour
½ teaspoon (2 mL) baking soda
1 cup (250 mL) finely chopped pecans

7½ dozen cookies

In large mixing bowl, combine sugar, butter, shortening, eggs and vanilla. Beat at medium speed of electric mixer until light and fluffy. Add flour and baking soda. Beat at low speed until soft dough forms. Stir in pecans.

Divide dough in half. Shape each half into 2-inch-diameter (5 cm) log. Wrap in plastic wrap or wax paper. Chill 2 to 3 hours, or until firm.

Heat oven to 350°F (180°C). Cut logs into ¼-inch (5 mm) slices. Place slices 2 inches (5 cm) apart on ungreased cookie sheets. Bake for 7 to 8 minutes, or until edges are light golden brown. Cool completely before storing.

Fruited Walnut Slices

1   cup (250 mL) packed brown sugar
1/2 cup (125 mL) butter or margarine, softened
1   egg
2   tablespoons (25 mL) milk
1   teaspoon (5 mL) vanilla
2   cups (500 mL) all-purpose flour
1/2 teaspoon (2 mL) cream of tartar
1/8 teaspoon (0.5 mL) baking soda
    Pinch of salt
1/2 cup (125 mL) chopped dates
1/2 cup (125 mL) finely chopped walnuts
1/4 cup (50 mL) golden raisins

About 4 1/2 dozen cookies

In large mixing bowl, combine sugar, butter, egg, milk and vanillla. Beat at medium speed of electric mixer until well blended. Add flour, cream of tartar, baking soda and salt. Beat at low speed until soft dough forms. Stir in dates, walnuts and raisins.

Divide dough in half. Shape each half into 1 1/2-inch-diameter (4 cm) log. Wrap in plastic wrap or wax paper. Chill 3 to 4 hours, or until firm.

Heat oven to 350°F (180°C). Lightly grease cookie sheets. Cut logs into 1/4-inch (5 mm) slices. Place slices 2 inches (5 cm) apart on prepared cookie sheets. Bake for 8 to 10 minutes, or until set. Cool completely before storing.

Refrigerated Cookies

Drop Cookies

Drop Cookie Basics

Drop cookie ingredients can be quickly combined and "dropped" from a spoon onto a cookie sheet. To shape drop cookies, follow the directions below. Typically, ordinary spoons are used, but some people prefer to use a small ice cream scoop to form drop cookies. Try to make all the cookies the same size and shape so they will finish baking at the same time.

Drop cookies are usually done when the edges and bottoms are golden brown or when a slight impression remains when the cookie is touched in the center (see page 10).

Cool the cookie sheets between bakings to keep the cookie dough from spreading too much.

How to Mix Drop Cookie Dough — 4 Basic Steps

1) Beat sugar, butter, eggs and flavorings in large mixing bowl until light and fluffy.

2) Combine dry ingredients (flour, baking powder, salt, etc.) in separate bowl, if desired.

3) Add dry ingredients to wet ingredients and beat until soft dough forms. (If dough becomes too stiff for an electric mixer, use a wooden spoon.)

4) Stir in large pieces, such as gumdrops, chocolate chips or nuts, with a wooden spoon.

How to Shape Drop Cookies

Shape drop cookies using two ordinary teaspoons or tablespoons (not measuring spoons), or one spoon and a rubber spatula. Scoop up the specified amount of dough with one spoon, then use the other spoon or spatula to push the dough onto the cookie sheet. Space the cookies about 2 inches (5 cm) apart on cookie sheets.

Use small ice cream scoops instead of spoons, if desired. Scoops are available at gourmet specialty shops. (A number 50 size works well.) Scrape the scoop on the side of mixing bowl before dropping dough on cookie sheet, for consistent cookie size.

Drop Cookies

Apple Raisin Cookies

1 cup (250 mL) sugar
1 cup (250 mL) unsweetened
   applesauce
1/2 cup (125 mL) vegetable
   shortening
1 egg
2 cups (500 mL) all-purpose
   flour
1 cup (250 mL) uncooked
   quick-cooking oats
1 teaspoon (5 mL) baking soda
1 teaspoon (5 mL) apple pie
   spice
1/2 teaspoon (2 mL) baking
   powder
1/4 teaspoon (1 mL) salt
1/2 cup (125 mL) raisins
1/2 cup (125 mL) chopped pecans

3 dozen cookies

Heat oven to 375°F (190°C). In large mixing bowl, combine sugar, applesauce, shortening and egg. Beat at medium speed of electric mixer until well blended. Add flour, oats, baking soda, apple pie spice, baking powder and salt. Beat at low speed until soft dough forms. Stir in raisins and pecans.

Drop dough by heaping tea-spoons 2 inches (5 cm) apart onto ungreased cookie sheets. Bake for 11 to 15 minutes, or until light golden brown. Cool completely before storing.

Drop Cookies

Cranberry Drops

- ½ cup (125 mL) granulated sugar
- ½ cup (125 mL) packed brown sugar
- ¼ cup (50 mL) butter or margarine, softened
- 1 egg
- 2 tablespoons (25 mL) milk
- 1 tablespoon (15 mL) orange juice
- ½ teaspoon (2 mL) vanilla
- 1½ cups (375 mL) all-purpose flour
- ½ teaspoon (2 mL) baking powder
- ¼ teaspoon (1 mL) baking soda
- ¼ teaspoon (1 mL) salt
- 1 cup (250 mL) dried cranberries

About 3 dozen cookies

Heat oven to 375°F (190°C). Lightly grease cookie sheets. Set aside. In large mixing bowl, combine sugars, butter, egg, milk, juice and vanilla. Beat at medium speed of electric mixer until well blended. Add flour, baking powder, baking soda and salt. Beat at low speed until soft dough forms. Stir in cranberries.

Drop dough by heaping tea-spoons 2 inches (5 cm) apart onto prepared cookie sheets. Bake for 8 to 12 minutes, or until golden brown. Cool completely before storing.

Pumpkin Date Cookies

1 1/2   *cups (375 mL) granulated sugar*
  1   *cup (250 mL) canned pumpkin*
 1/2   *cup (125 mL) butter or margarine, softened*
  1   *egg*
  1   *teaspoon (5 mL) vanilla*
2 3/4   *cups (675 mL) all-purpose flour*
  1   *teaspoon (5 mL) baking powder*
  1   *teaspoon (5 mL) baking soda*
  1   *teaspoon (5 mL) ground cinnamon*
 1/2   *teaspoon (2 mL) ground nutmeg*
 1/2   *teaspoon (2 mL) salt*
  1   *pkg. (8 oz./227 g) chopped dates*

Frosting:

 3/4   *cup (175 mL) packed brown sugar*
 1/4   *cup (50 mL) butter or margarine, softened*
1 1/4   *cups (300 mL) powdered sugar*
  1   *to 2 tablespoons (15 to 25 mL) half-and-half*
  1   *teaspoon (5 mL) vanilla*

 1/2   *cup (125 mL) finely chopped pecans*

3 1/2 dozen cookies

Heat oven to 375°F (190°C). Lightly grease cookie sheets. Set aside. In large mixing bowl, combine granulated sugar, pumpkin, 1/2 cup (125 mL) butter, the egg and 1 teaspoon (5 mL) vanilla. Beat at medium speed of electric mixer until well blended. Add flour, baking powder, baking soda, cinnamon, nutmeg and salt. Beat at low speed until soft dough forms. Stir in dates.

Drop dough by heaping teaspoons 2 inches (5 cm) apart onto prepared cookie sheets. Bake for 10 to 12 minutes, or until set. Cool completely.

In 1-quart (1 L) saucepan, combine brown sugar and 1/4 cup (50 mL) butter. Cook over medium heat until butter is melted and mixture can be stirred smooth, stirring constantly. Remove from heat. Add remaining frosting ingredients. Stir until smooth. Spread frosting evenly on cookies. Sprinkle tops with pecans. Let dry completely before storing.

Raisin Spice Cookies

1¹/₄ cups (300 mL) water
1 cup (250 mL) raisins
1 cup (250 mL) granulated
  sugar
1 cup (250 mL) vegetable
  shortening
¹/₂ cup (125 mL) light molasses
1 egg
4 cups (1 L) all-purpose flour
2 teaspoons (10 mL) baking
  soda
1 teaspoon (5 mL) ground
  cinnamon
1 teaspoon (5 mL) ground
  ginger
¹/₂ teaspoon (2 mL) ground
  cloves
¹/₄ teaspoon (1 mL) salt

Frosting:
1 cup (250 mL) powdered
  sugar
¹/₄ cup (50 mL) butter or
  margarine, softened
1 to 2 tablespoons (15 to
  25 mL) milk

4¹/₂ dozen cookies

Heat oven to 375°F (190°C). Lightly grease cookie sheets. Set aside. In 1-quart (1 L) saucepan, combine water and raisins. Bring to boil over medium-high heat. Boil for 1 minute. Drain, reserving liquid. Set raisins aside.

In large mixing bowl, combine reserved raisin liquid, granulated sugar, shortening, molasses and egg. Beat at medium speed of electric mixer until well blended. Add raisins, flour, baking soda, cinnamon, ginger, cloves and salt. Beat at low speed of electric mixer until soft dough forms.

Drop dough by heaping teaspoons 2 inches (5 cm) apart onto prepared cookie sheets. Bake for 8 to 10 minutes, or until light golden brown. Cool completely.

In small mixing bowl, combine frosting ingredients. Beat at low speed of electric mixer until smooth. Spread frosting evenly on cookies. Let dry completely before storing.

Microwave tip: In 4-cup (1 L) measure, combine water and raisins. Cover with plastic wrap. Microwave at High for 3¹/₂ to 5 minutes, or until boiling. Let stand for 3 to 5 minutes to plump. Carefully remove plastic wrap and discard. Drain, reserving liquid. Continue as directed.

Drop Cookies

Coconut Macadamia Cookies

1/2 cup (125 mL) granulated
   sugar
1/2 cup (125 mL) packed brown
   sugar
1/2 cup (125 mL) butter or
   margarine, softened
1 egg
1 teaspoon (5 mL) vanilla
1 1/4 cups (300 mL) all-purpose
   flour
1 cup (250 mL) uncooked
   quick-cooking oats
1/2 cup (125 mL) flaked coconut
1/2 teaspoon (2 mL) baking soda
1/4 teaspoon (1 mL) salt
1 cup (250 mL) coarsely
   chopped macadamia nuts

3 dozen cookies

Heat oven to 350°F (180°C).
Lightly grease cookie sheets.
Set aside. In large mixing
bowl, combine sugars, butter,
egg and vanilla. Beat at medium speed of electric mixer
until light and fluffy. Add
flour, oats, coconut, baking
soda and salt. Beat at low
speed until soft dough forms.
Stir in nuts.

Drop dough by heaping teaspoons 2 inches (5 cm) apart
onto prepared cookie sheets.
Bake for 7 to 10 minutes, or
until edges are light golden
brown. Let cool for 1 minute
before removing from cookie
sheets. Cool completely before
storing.

Chocolate Swirls

1/2 cup (125 mL) granulated
   sugar
1/2 cup (125 mL) packed brown
   sugar
1/2 cup (125 mL) butter or
   margarine, softened
1 pkg. (3 oz./85 g) cream
   cheese, softened
1 egg
1 teaspoon (5 mL) vanilla
2 cups (500 mL) all-purpose
   flour
1/2 teaspoon (2 mL) baking
   powder
1/4 teaspoon (1 mL) salt
1 cup (250 mL) semisweet
   chocolate chips, melted and
   slightly cooled

4 dozen cookies

Heat oven to 350°F (180°C). In
large mixing bowl, combine
sugars, butter, cream cheese,
egg and vanilla. Beat at medium speed of electric mixer
until light and fluffy. Add
flour, baking powder and salt.
Beat at low speed until soft
dough forms. Fold melted
chips into dough until lightly
marbled. (Do not overmix.)

Drop dough by heaping teaspoons 2 inches (5 cm) apart
onto ungreased cookie sheets.
Bake for 10 to 12 minutes, or
until edges are light golden
brown. Cool completely
before storing.

Drop Cookies

Monster Cookies

1 cup (250 mL) packed brown sugar
³/4 cup (175 mL) vegetable shortening
¹/4 cup (50 mL) water
1 egg
1 teaspoon (5 mL) vanilla
3 cups (750 mL) uncooked old-fashioned rolled
    oats
1 cup (250 mL) all-purpose flour
³/4 teaspoon (4 mL) salt
¹/2 teaspoon (2 mL) baking soda
1 cup (250 mL) candy-coated plain chocolate pieces
¹/2 cup (125 mL) chopped nuts (optional)

¹/2 dozen cookies

Heat oven to 350°F (180°C). In large mixing bowl, combine sugar, shortening, water, egg and vanilla. Beat at medium speed of electric mixer until well blended. Add oats, flour, salt and baking soda. Beat at low speed until soft dough forms. Stir in chocolate pieces and nuts.

Drop dough by scant cups (250 mL) 4 inches (10 cm) apart onto ungreased cookie sheets. Flatten dough to ¹/2-inch (1 cm) thickness with back of spoon. Bake for 18 to 20 minutes, or until golden brown. Let cool for 5 minutes before removing from cookie sheets. Cool completely before storing.

Drop Cookies

Choco-Cherry Macaroons

6 cups (1.5 L) flaked coconut
1 can (14 oz./396 g)
    sweetened condensed milk
1 teaspoon (5 mL) almond
    extract
1 cup (250 mL) miniature
    semisweet chocolate chips
1/2 cup (125 mL) chopped
    maraschino cherries, well
    drained

About 3 dozen cookies

Heat oven to 350°F (180°C). Line cookie sheets with parchment paper. Set aside. In large mixing bowl, combine coconut, milk and almond extract. Stir until coconut is well coated. Stir in chips and cherries.

Drop dough by heaping teaspoons 2 inches (5 cm) apart onto prepared cookie sheets. Bake for 7 to 8 minutes, or until edges are golden brown. Cool completely before storing.

Tip: Parchment paper is necessary for success with this recipe. Parchment paper can be reused if crumbs are scraped off paper.

Oatmeal Prune Cookies

- 1/2 cup (125 mL) granulated sugar
- 1/2 cup (125 mL) packed brown sugar
- 1/2 cup (125 mL) coarsely chopped pitted prunes
- 1/4 cup (50 mL) orange juice
- 1 teaspoon (5 mL) vanilla
- 1 1/4 cups (300 mL) all-purpose flour
- 1 1/4 cups (300 mL) uncooked quick-cooking oats
- 1/2 teaspoon (2 mL) baking powder
- 1/2 teaspoon (2 mL) baking soda
- 1/4 teaspoon (1 mL) salt

2 dozen cookies

Heat oven to 350°F (180°C). Lightly grease cookie sheets. Set aside. In large mixing bowl, combine sugars, prunes, juice and vanilla. Beat at medium speed of electric mixer until well blended. Add remaining ingredients. Beat at low speed until soft dough forms.

Drop dough by heaping teaspoons 2 inches (5 cm) apart onto prepared cookie sheets. Bake for 10 to 12 minutes, or until set. Let cool for 1 minute before removing from cookie sheets. Cool completely before storing.

Date Ginger Cookies

1 pkg. (8 oz./227 g) chopped dates
1/2 cup (125 mL) water
1 cup (250 mL) sugar
1 cup (250 mL) vegetable shortening
1/2 cup (125 mL) light molasses
1 egg
3 3/4 cups (925 mL) all-purpose flour
2 teaspoons (10 mL) baking soda
1/2 to 1 teaspoon (2 to 5 mL) ground ginger
1/2 teaspoon (2 mL) salt

5 dozen cookies

In 1-quart (1 L) saucepan, combine dates and water. Bring to boil over medium-high heat. Reduce heat to low. Simmer for 2 to 4 minutes, or until dates are softened. Remove from heat. Cool to room temperature. Set date mixture aside.

Heat oven to 350°F (180°C). Lightly grease cookie sheets. Set aside. In large mixing bowl, combine sugar, shortening, molasses and egg. Beat at medium speed of electric mixer until well blended. Add date mixture. Beat at low speed until combined. Add remaining ingredients. Beat at low speed until soft dough forms.

Drop dough by heaping teaspoons 2 inches (5 cm) apart onto prepared cookie sheets. Bake for 12 to 14 minutes, or until set. Cool completely before storing. If desired, frost cookies with favorite frosting.

Drop Cookies

Root Beer Float Cookies

1 cup (250 mL) granulated sugar
1 cup (250 mL) packed brown sugar
1 cup (250 mL) butter or margarine, softened
½ cup (125 mL) buttermilk
2 eggs
2 teaspoons (10 mL) root beer extract
1 teaspoon (5 mL) vanilla
4 cups (1 L) all-purpose flour
1 teaspoon (5 mL) baking soda
¼ teaspoon (1 mL) salt

Frosting:

1 cup (250 mL) powdered sugar
1 tablespoon (15 mL) half-and-half
2 teaspoons (10 mL) butter or margarine,
   softened
1 teaspoon (5 mL) root beer extract

Heat oven to 375°F (190°C). Lightly grease cookie sheets. Set aside. In large mixing bowl, combine granulated sugar, brown sugar, 1 cup (250 mL) butter, the buttermilk, eggs, 2 teaspoons (10 mL) root beer extract and the vanilla. Beat at medium speed of electric mixer until well blended. Add flour, baking soda and salt. Beat at low speed until soft dough forms.

Drop dough by heaping teaspoons 2 inches (5 cm) apart onto prepared cookie sheets. Bake for 10 to 12 minutes, or until set. Cool completely.

In small mixing bowl, combine frosting ingredients. Beat at low speed of electric mixer until smooth. Spread frosting evenly on cookies. Let dry completely before storing.

5 dozen cookies

Drop Cookies

Peanut Butter Banana Cookies

3/4 cup (175 mL) packed brown sugar
1/2 cup (125 mL) butter or margarine, softened
1/4 cup (50 mL) chunky peanut butter
1 egg
1/2 teaspoon (2 mL) vanilla
3/4 cup (175 mL) mashed bananas (2 small)
3 cups (750 mL) all-purpose flour
1 teaspoon (5 mL) baking soda
1/4 teaspoon (1 mL) salt

Frosting:
1 cup (250 mL) powdered sugar
1/4 cup (50 mL) butter or margarine, softened
1 square (1 oz./30 g) unsweetened baking
   chocolate, melted and slightly cooled
1 to 2 tablespoons (15 to 25 mL) milk

Heat oven to 350°F (180°C). Lightly grease cookie sheets. Set aside. In large mixing bowl, combine brown sugar, 1/2 cup (125 mL) butter, the peanut butter, egg and vanilla. Beat at medium speed of electric mixer until light and fluffy. Add bananas. Beat at low speed just until combined. Add flour, baking soda and salt. Beat at low speed until soft dough forms.

Drop dough by heaping teaspoons 2 inches (5 cm) apart onto prepared cookie sheets. Bake for 10 to 12 minutes, or until set. Cool completely.

In small mixing bowl, combine frosting ingredients. Beat at low speed of electric mixer until smooth. Spread frosting evenly on cookies. Let dry completely before storing.

About 4 dozen cookies

Drop Cookies

Orange Poppy Seed Drops

  1 cup (250 mL) granulated
       sugar
 3/4 cup (175 mL) butter or
       margarine, softened
  2 eggs
2 1/2 cups (625 mL) all-purpose
       flour
  2 teaspoons (10 mL) grated
       orange peel
  1 tablespoon (15 mL) orange
       juice
  1 tablespoon (15 mL) poppy
       seed
 1/2 teaspoon (2 mL) baking soda
 1/2 teaspoon (2 mL) ground
       ginger

Frosting:

 1/2 cup (125 mL) powdered
       sugar
  2 to 3 teaspoons (10 to 15 mL)
       orange juice

                    3 dozen cookies

Heat oven to 350°F (180°C).
Lightly grease cookie sheets.
Set aside. In large mixing bowl,
combine granulated sugar, butter and eggs. Beat at medium
speed of electric mixer until
well blended. Add flour, peel,
1 tablespoon (15 mL) juice, the
poppy seed, baking soda and
ginger. Beat at low speed until
soft dough forms.

Drop dough by heaping teaspoons 2 inches (5 cm) apart
onto prepared cookie sheets.
Bake for 10 to 15 minutes, or
until edges are golden brown.
Cool completely.

In small mixing bowl, combine frosting ingredients. Stir
until smooth. Spread frosting
evenly on cookies. Let dry
completely before storing.

Toffee Apple Cookies

1⅓ cups (325 mL) packed
    brown sugar
½ cup (125 mL) butter or
    margarine, softened
¼ cup (50 mL) unsweetened
    applesauce
1 egg
2½ cups (625 mL) all-purpose
    flour
1 teaspoon (5 mL) baking soda
½ teaspoon (2 mL) salt
1 pkg. (7.5 oz./213 g) English
    toffee bits
1 cup (250 mL) coarsely
    chopped cooking apple
½ cup (125 mL) chopped pecans

4 dozen cookies

Heat oven to 375°F (190°C).
Lightly grease cookie sheets.
Set aside. In large mixing bowl,
combine sugar, butter, applesauce and egg. Beat at medium
speed of electric mixer until
well blended. Add flour, baking
soda and salt. Beat at low speed
until soft dough forms. Stir in
bits, apple and pecans.

Drop dough by heaping teaspoons 2 inches (5 cm) apart
onto prepared cookie sheets.
Bake for 12 to 14 minutes, or
until edges are golden brown.
Cool completely before storing.

Drop Cookies

Chocolaty Drop Cookies

½ cup (125 mL) granulated
    sugar
½ cup (125 mL) packed brown
    sugar
½ cup (125 mL) butter or
    margarine, softened
½ cup (125 mL) vegetable
    shortening
1 egg
2 cups (500 mL) all-purpose
    flour
¼ cup (50 mL) unsweetened
    cocoa
¼ cup (50 mL) milk
1½ teaspoons (7 mL) vanilla
1 teaspoon (5 mL) salt
½ teaspoon (2 mL) baking
    powder
½ teaspoon (2 mL) baking soda
¾ cup (175 mL) miniature
    candy-coated semisweet
    chocolate pieces

4 dozen cookies

Heat oven to 350°F (180°C). In
large mixing bowl, combine
sugars, butter, shortening and
egg. Beat at medium speed of
electric mixer until light and
fluffy. Add flour, cocoa, milk,
vanilla, salt, baking powder
and baking soda. Beat at low
speed until soft dough forms.
Stir in chocolate pieces.

Drop dough by heaping teaspoons 2 inches (5 cm) apart
onto ungreased cookie sheets.
Bake for 9 to 10 minutes, or
until set. Cool completely
before storing.

Cranberry Haystacks

  1 *pkg. (3 oz./85 g) cream cheese, softened*
  2 *tablespoons (25 mL) milk*
  2 *squares (1 oz./30 g each) white baking*
     chocolate, melted and slightly cooled
 1/2 *teaspoon (2 mL) vanilla*
 1/4 *teaspoon (1 mL) salt*
  2 *cups (500 mL) miniature marshmallows*
1 1/2 *cups (375 mL) chow mein noodles*
 1/3 *cup (75 mL) dried cranberries*

Line cookie sheets with wax paper. Set aside. In medium mixing bowl, combine cream cheese and milk. Beat at medium speed of electric mixer until smooth. Add melted chocolate, vanilla and salt. Beat at medium speed until smooth.

Stir in marshmallows, noodles and cranberries. Drop mixture by heaping teaspoons onto prepared cookie sheets. Chill until set. Store in refrigerator.

1 1/2 dozen cookies

Drop Cookies

Coconut Date Macaroons

2   *egg whites*
1/2   *cup (125 mL) sugar*
2   *tablespoons (25 mL)*
      all-purpose flour
1/4   *teaspoon (1 mL) salt*
1/4   *teaspoon (1 mL) almond*
      extract
2   *cups (500 mL) flaked coconut*
1/2   *cup (125 mL) chopped dates*
1/4   *cup (50 mL) chopped*
      almonds

About 1 dozen cookies

Heat oven to 325°F (160°C). Lightly grease cookie sheets. Set aside. Place egg whites in medium mixing bowl. Beat at medium speed of electric mixer until foamy. Add sugar, flour, salt and almond extract. Beat until well blended. Stir in coconut, dates and almonds.

Drop dough by heaping teaspoons 2 inches (5 cm) apart onto prepared cookie sheets. Bake for 13 to 17 minutes, or until set and golden brown. Cool completely before storing.

Chocolate Brownie Cookies

2 cups (500 mL) sugar
1 cup (250 mL) vegetable oil
4 eggs
4 squares (1 oz./30 g each)
    unsweetened baking
    chocolate, melted and
    slightly cooled
2 teaspoons (10 mL) vanilla
4 cups (1 L) all-purpose flour
2 teaspoons (10 mL) baking
    soda
1/2 teaspoon (2 mL) salt
1/2 cup (125 mL) chopped
    walnuts

5 dozen cookies

Heat oven to 350°F (180°C).
Lightly grease cookie sheets.
Set aside. In large mixing bowl,
combine sugar, oil, eggs, melted
chocolate and vanilla. Beat at
medium speed of electric mixer
until well blended. Add flour,
baking soda and salt. Beat at
low speed until soft dough
forms. Stir in walnuts.

Drop dough by heaping teaspoons 2 inches (5 cm) apart
onto prepared cookie sheets.
Bake for 10 to 12 minutes, or
until set. Cool completely
before storing.

Drop Cookies

Peanut Butterscotch Crispies

1 cup (250 mL) butterscotch chips
1/2 cup (125 mL) light corn syrup
2 tablespoons (25 mL) butter or margarine
1 cup (250 mL) creamy peanut butter
5 cups (1.25 L) whole-grain wheat flakes
1/2 cup (125 mL) chocolate-covered raisins
1/2 cup (125 mL) salted peanuts

3 dozen cookies

Line cookie sheets with wax paper. Set aside. In 3-quart (3 L) saucepan, combine chips, corn syrup and butter. Cook over medium heat until chips are melted, stirring constantly. Remove from heat. Stir in peanut butter. Add wheat flakes, raisins and peanuts. Stir to coat. Drop mixture by heaping teaspoons onto prepared cookie sheets. Cool completely before storing.

Drop Cookies

Spicy Gumdrop Cookies

3/4 cup (175 mL) packed brown
    sugar
1/2 cup (125 mL) granulated
    sugar
1/2 cup (125 mL) butter or
    margarine, softened
1/2 cup (125 mL) vegetable
    shortening
1 egg
1 teaspoon (5 mL) vanilla
2 cups (500 mL) all-purpose
    flour
2 cups (500 mL) uncooked
    quick-cooking oats
1/2 cup (125 mL) flaked coconut
1 teaspoon (5 mL) baking soda
1/2 teaspoon (2 mL) baking
    powder
1/4 teaspoon (1 mL) salt
1 cup (250 mL) chopped
    spiced gumdrops

3 1/2 dozen cookies

Heat oven to 375°F (190°C).
Lightly grease cookie sheets.
Set aside. In large mixing bowl,
combine sugars, butter, shortening, egg and vanilla. Beat at
medium speed of electric mixer
until light and fluffy. Add flour,
oats, coconut, baking soda,
baking powder and salt. Beat
at low speed until soft dough
forms. Stir in gumdrops.

Drop dough by heaping teaspoons 2 inches (5 cm) apart
onto prepared cookie sheets.
Bake for 7 to 10 minutes, or until
edges are golden brown. Let
cool for 1 minute before removing from cookie sheets. Cool
completely before storing.

Drop Cookies

Chocolate Cherry Drops

1 cup (250 mL) packed brown
    sugar
1/2 cup (125 mL) butter or
    margarine, softened
1/2 cup (125 mL) sour cream
3 squares (1 oz./30 g each)
    unsweetened baking
    chocolate, melted
1 egg
1 teaspoon (5 mL) vanilla
2 cups (500 mL) all-purpose flour
1/2 teaspoon (2 mL) baking soda
1/4 teaspoon (1 mL) salt
1/2 cup (125 mL) chopped
    maraschino cherries, drained
    (reserve 2 to 3 tablespoons/
    25 to 50 mL juice)

Frosting:
1 cup (250 mL) powdered sugar
1 square (1 oz./30 g)
    unsweetened baking chocolate,
    melted
2 tablespoons (25 mL) sour cream
1 tablespoon (15 mL) butter or
    margarine, melted

About 4 dozen cookies

Heat oven to 375°F (190°C).
Lightly grease cookie sheets.
Set aside. In large mixing bowl,
combine brown sugar, 1/2 cup
(125 mL) butter, 1/2 cup (125 mL)
sour cream, 3 squares melted
chocolate, the egg and vanilla.
Beat at medium speed of electric mixer until well blended.
Add flour, baking soda and
salt. Beat at low speed until
soft dough forms. Stir in cherries. Drop dough by heaping
teaspoons 2 inches (5 cm) apart
onto prepared cookie sheets.
Bake for 12 to 15 minutes, or
until set. Cool completely.

In medium mixing bowl, combine frosting ingredients and
reserved juice. Beat at low
speed of electric mixer until
smooth. Spread frosting evenly on cookies. Let dry completely before storing.

Drop Cookies

Crunchy Cashew Drops

1 cup (250 mL) packed brown
    sugar
3/4 cup (175 mL) butter or
    margarine, softened
1 egg
1 teaspoon (5 mL) vanilla
2 cups (500 mL) all-purpose
    flour
1/2 teaspoon (2 mL) baking
    powder
1/2 teaspoon (2 mL) baking soda
1/4 teaspoon (1 mL) salt
1 1/2 cups (375 mL) coarsely
    chopped cashews

Frosting:

2 cups (500 mL) powdered
    sugar
1/4 cup (50 mL) butter or
    margarine, softened
2 to 3 tablespoons (25 to 50 mL)
    half-and-half
1/2 teaspoon (2 mL) vanilla

3 1/2 dozen cookies

Heat oven to 375°F (190°C). In large mixing bowl, combine brown sugar, 3/4 cup (175 mL) butter, the egg and 1 teaspoon (5 mL) vanilla. Beat at medium speed of electric mixer until light and fluffy. Add flour, baking powder, baking soda and salt. Beat at low speed until soft dough forms. Stir in cashews.

Drop dough by heaping teaspoons 2 inches (5 cm) apart onto ungreased cookie sheets. Bake for 8 to 10 minutes, or until edges are light golden brown. Cool completely.

In medium mixing bowl, combine frosting ingredients. Beat at low speed of electric mixer until smooth. Spread frosting evenly on cookies. Let dry completely before storing.

Orange Hazelnut Cookies

½ cup (125 mL) granulated sugar
½ cup (125 mL) packed brown sugar
½ cup (125 mL) butter or margarine, softened
½ cup (125 mL) semisweet chocolate chips,
   melted and slightly cooled
1 egg
2 teaspoons (10 mL) grated orange peel
1 teaspoon (5 mL) vanilla
2 cups (500 mL) all-purpose flour
¾ teaspoon (4 mL) baking soda
¼ teaspoon (1 mL) salt
½ cup (125 mL) chopped hazelnuts

3 dozen cookies

Heat oven to 350°F (180°C). In large mixing bowl, combine sugars, butter, melted chips, egg, peel and vanilla. Beat at medium speed of electric mixer until well blended. Add flour, baking soda and salt. Beat at low speed until soft dough forms. Stir in hazelnuts.

Drop dough by heaping teaspoons 2 inches (5 cm) apart onto ungreased cookie sheets. Bake for 10 to 12 minutes, or until set. Cool completely before storing.

Oatmeal Raisin Cookies

1¼ cups (300 mL) packed brown sugar
½ cup (125 mL) vegetable shortening
¼ cup (50 mL) butter or margarine, softened
¼ cup (50 mL) water
1 egg
1½ teaspoons (7 mL) vanilla
3 cups (750 mL) uncooked quick-cooking oats
1 cup (250 mL) all-purpose flour
½ cup (125 mL) flaked coconut
½ teaspoon (2 mL) baking soda
½ teaspoon (2 mL) ground cinnamon
½ teaspoon (2 mL) salt
1 cup (250 mL) raisins
½ cup (125 mL) chopped walnuts

About 3½ dozen cookies

Heat oven to 375°F (190°C). Lightly grease cookie sheets. Set aside. In large mixing bowl, combine sugar, shortening, butter, water, egg and vanilla. Beat at medium speed of electric mixer until well blended. Add oats, flour, coconut, baking soda, cinnamon and salt. Beat at low speed until soft dough forms. Stir in raisins and walnuts.

Drop dough by heaping teaspoons 2 inches (5 cm) apart onto prepared cookie sheets. Bake for 8 to 10 minutes, or until golden brown. Cool completely before storing.

Drop Cookies

Blueberry Lemon Drops

2 cups (500 mL) plus
  1 tablespoon (15 mL)
  all-purpose flour, divided
1 cup (250 mL) fresh
  blueberries
1 cup (250 mL) sugar
½ cup (125 mL) butter or
  margarine, softened
1 egg
1 teaspoon (5 mL) grated
  lemon peel
1 tablespoon (15 mL) fresh
  lemon juice
1 teaspoon (5 mL) baking
  powder
½ teaspoon (2 mL) baking soda
½ teaspoon (2 mL) salt

2 dozen cookies

Heat oven to 375°F (190°C). Lightly grease cookie sheets. Set aside. In small mixing bowl, combine 1 tablespoon (15 mL) flour and the blueberries. Toss to coat. Set aside.

In large mixing bowl, combine sugar, butter, egg, peel and juice. Beat at medium speed of electric mixer until light and fluffy. Add remaining 2 cups (500 mL) flour, the baking powder, baking soda and salt. Beat at low speed until soft dough forms. Gently fold in blueberries.

Drop dough by heaping tea-spoons 2 inches (5 cm) apart onto prepared cookie sheets. Bake for 11 to 13 minutes, or until edges are golden brown. Cool completely before storing.

Apricot Jewel Cookies

1 cup (250 mL) butter or
   margarine, softened
$1/2$ cup (125 mL) granulated
   sugar
$1/2$ cup (125 mL) packed brown
   sugar
1 egg
1 teaspoon (5 mL) vanilla
$21/2$ cups (625 mL) all-purpose
   flour
$1/4$ cup (50 mL) orange juice
1 teaspoon (5 mL) baking soda
$1/2$ teaspoon (2 mL) salt
1 pkg. (6 oz./170 g) dried
   apricots, chopped
$1/2$ cup (125 mL) chopped
   cashews

$4^{1/2}$ dozen cookies

Heat oven to 350°F (180°C). In large mixing bowl, combine butter, sugars, egg and vanilla. Beat at medium speed of electric mixer until light and fluffy. Add flour, juice, baking soda and salt. Beat at low speed until soft dough forms. Stir in apricots and cashews.

Drop dough by heaping teaspoons 2 inches (5 cm) apart onto ungreased cookie sheets. Bake for 9 to 10 minutes, or until edges are golden brown. Cool completely before storing.

Tip: Dried peaches can be substituted for dried apricots.

Carrot Orange Cookies

½ cup (125 mL) granulated sugar
½ cup (125 mL) butter or margarine, softened
1 egg
2 tablespoons (25 mL) orange juice
1 teaspoon (5 mL) vanilla
1 cup (250 mL) all-purpose flour
1 cup (250 mL) uncooked quick-cooking oats
¾ cup (175 mL) grated carrot
1 teaspoon (5 mL) baking powder
¼ teaspoon (1 mL) baking soda
¼ teaspoon (1 mL) salt
½ cup (125 mL) chopped pecans

Drizzle:
1 cup (250 mL) powdered sugar
½ teaspoon (2 mL) grated orange peel
3 to 4 teaspoons (15 to 20 mL) orange juice

About 3 dozen cookies

Heat oven to 350°F (180°C). Lightly grease cookie sheets. Set aside. In large mixing bowl, combine granulated sugar, butter, egg, 2 tablespoons (25 mL) juice and the vanilla. Beat at medium speed of electric mixer until well blended. Add flour, oats, carrot, baking powder, baking soda and salt. Beat at low speed until soft dough forms. Stir in pecans.

Drop dough by heaping teaspoons 2 inches (5 cm) apart onto prepared cookie sheets. Bake for 8 to 12 minutes, or until light golden brown. Cool completely.

In small mixing bowl, combine drizzle ingredients. Stir until smooth. Pipe or drizzle mixture over cookies. Let dry completely before storing.

Drop Cookies

Carrot Cake Cookies

1 cup (250 mL) granulated sugar
1 cup (250 mL) packed brown sugar
1/2 cup (125 mL) butter or margarine, softened
1/2 cup (125 mL) vegetable shortening
2 eggs
1 teaspoon (5 mL) vanilla
3 cups (750 mL) all-purpose flour
1 teaspoon (5 mL) baking powder
1/2 teaspoon (2 mL) baking soda
1/2 teaspoon (2 mL) ground cinnamon
1/4 teaspoon (1 mL) salt
1 can (8 oz./227 g) crushed pineapple, drained
   (reserve 1 to 2 tablespoons/15 to 25 mL juice)
1/2 cup (125 mL) grated carrot
1/2 cup (125 mL) golden raisins
1/2 cup (125 mL) chopped nuts

Frosting:

2 cups (500 mL) powdered sugar
1 pkg. (3 oz./85 g) cream cheese, softened
1 tablespoon (15 mL) butter or margarine, softened

4 1/2 dozen cookies

Heat oven to 375°F (190°C). Lightly grease cookie sheets. Set aside. In large mixing bowl, combine granulated sugar, brown sugar, 1/2 cup (125 mL) butter, the shortening, eggs and vanilla. Beat at medium speed of electric mixer until well blended. Add flour, baking powder, baking soda, cinnamon and salt. Beat at low speed until soft dough forms. Stir in pineapple, carrot, raisins and nuts.

Drop dough by heaping teaspoons 2 inches (5 cm) apart onto prepared baking sheets. Bake for 10 to 12 minutes, or until light golden brown. Cool completely.

In small mixing bowl, combine frosting ingredients and reserved juice. Beat at low speed of electric mixer until smooth. Spread frosting evenly on cookies. Let dry completely before storing.

Chocolate Chip Cookies

Chocolate Chip Cookie Basics

Chocolate chip cookies are a special kind of drop cookie that have become the most popular made-from-scratch cookie in North America. The most famous recipe for chocolate chip cookies is the legendary Nestlé® Toll House® Cookie, named after an old toll house on the outskirts of Whitman, Massachusetts. In about 1930,

Mrs. Wakefield, the owner of this historic house, was experimenting with a favorite butter cookie and found that adding a chopped bar of Nestlé Semi-Sweet Chocolate to the dough added a delicious new dimension to the cookies. Since then, Nestlé has developed small bits of chocolate that we know as semisweet

Semisweet chocolate chips

Miniature semisweet chocolate chips

Milk chocolate chips

Butterscotch chips

Peanut butter chips

Candy-coated semisweet chocolate chips

Candy-coated plain or semisweet chocolate pieces

chocolate morsels, or chips. Over the years, the chocolate chip phenomenon has grown; today there is an extensive variety of chips to choose from. There are semisweet chocolate chips, miniature chocolate chips, milk chocolate chips, vanilla baking chips, mint chocolate chips, rainbow chips, butterscotch chips, peanut butter chips and candy-coated chocolate chips. If you get tired of chips, try candy-coated chocolate pieces, semisweet chocolate chunks, white chocolate chunks or milk chocolate chunks. Most chips are interchangeable, so if you can't find the variety called for in a recipe, try another.

Vanilla baking chips

Mint chocolate chips

Rainbow semisweet chocolate chips

Semisweet chocolate chunks

White chocolate chunks

Milk chocolate chunks

Chocolate Chip Cookies

Original Nestlé® Toll House® Chocolate Chip Cookies

2 1/4 cups (550 mL) all-purpose flour
  1 teaspoon (5 mL) baking soda
  1 teaspoon (5 mL) salt
  1 cup (250 mL) butter, softened
  3/4 cup (175 mL) granulated sugar
  3/4 cup (175 mL) packed brown sugar
  1 teaspoon (5 mL) vanilla
  2 eggs
  1 pkg. (12 oz./341 g) Nestlé® Toll House®
    Semi-Sweet Chocolate Morsels
  1 cup (250 mL) chopped nuts

5 dozen cookies

Heat oven to 375°F (190°C). In small mixing bowl, combine flour, baking soda and salt. Set aside. In large mixing bowl, combine butter, sugars and vanilla. Beat at medium speed of electric mixer until light and fluffy. Beat in eggs. Add flour mixture. Beat at low speed until soft dough forms. Stir in Nestlé® Toll House® Semi-Sweet Chocolate Morsels and nuts.

Drop dough by heaping teaspoons 2 inches (5 cm) apart onto ungreased cookie sheets. Bake for 9 to 11 minutes, or until edges are golden brown. Cool completely before storing.

Toll House® is a registered trademark of Nestlé Food Company.

Nestlé® is a registered trademark of Société des Produits Nestlé, S.A.

Nestlé® Toll House® Chocolate Chip Oat Cookies

1¼ cups (300 mL) packed brown sugar
  1 cup (250 mL) butter or margarine, softened
  ½ cup (125 mL) granulated sugar
  2 eggs
  2 tablespoons (25 mL) milk
  2 teaspoons (10 mL) vanilla
1¾ cups (425 mL) all-purpose flour
  1 teaspoon (5 mL) baking soda
  ½ teaspoon (2 mL) salt (optional)
2½ cups (625 mL) uncooked quick-cooking or
    old-fashioned rolled oats
  1 pkg. (12 oz./341 g) Nestlé® Toll House®
    Semi-Sweet Chocolate Morsels
  1 cup (250 mL) coarsely chopped nuts (optional)

About 5 dozen cookies

Heat oven to 375°F (190°C). In large mixing bowl, combine brown sugar, butter and granulated sugar. Beat at medium speed of electric mixer until light and fluffy. Add eggs, milk and vanilla. Beat at medium speed until well blended. Add flour, baking soda and salt. Beat at low speed until soft dough forms. Stir in oats, Nestlé® Toll House® Semi-Sweet Chocolate Morsels and nuts.

Drop dough by heaping teaspoons 2 inches (5 cm) apart onto ungreased cookie sheets. Bake for 9 to 10 minutes for a chewy cookie or 12 to 13 minutes for a crisp cookie. Let cool for 1 minute before removing from cookie sheets. Cool completely before storing.

Toll House® is a registered trademark of Nestlé Food Company.

Nestlé® is a registered trademark of Société des Produits Nestlé, S.A.

Chocolate Chip Cookies

Chocolate Chocolate Chip Cookies

1/2 cup (125 mL) granulated sugar
1/2 cup (125 mL) packed brown sugar
1/2 cup (125 mL) butter or margarine, softened
2 eggs
1/2 teaspoon (2 mL) vanilla
1 3/4 cups (425 mL) all-purpose flour
1/4 cup (50 mL) unsweetened cocoa
1 teaspoon (5 mL) baking soda
1/4 teaspoon (1 mL) salt
1 cup (250 mL) semisweet chocolate chips
1 cup (250 mL) coarsely chopped walnuts

2 1/2 dozen cookies

Heat oven to 375°F (190°C). In large mixing bowl, combine sugars, butter, eggs and vanilla. Beat at medium speed of electric mixer until well blended. Add flour, cocoa, baking soda and salt. Beat at low speed until soft dough forms. Stir in chips and walnuts.

Drop dough by heaping tablespoons 3 inches (8 cm) apart onto ungreased cookie sheets. Bake for 8 to 10 minutes, or until set. Let cool for 1 minute before removing from cookie sheets. Cool completely before storing.

Peanut Butter Candy Cookies

    1 cup (250 mL) packed brown
        sugar
  1/2 cup (125 mL) granulated
        sugar
  1/2 cup (125 mL) butter or
        margarine, softened
  1/2 cup (125 mL) vegetable
        shortening
    2 eggs
1 1/2 teaspoons (7 mL) vanilla
    3 cups (750 mL) all-purpose
        flour
1 1/2 cups (375 mL) cornflakes
    1 teaspoon (5 mL) baking soda
  1/4 teaspoon (1 mL) salt
    1 pkg. (8 oz./227 g) candy-
        coated peanut butter pieces
  1/2 cup (125 mL) coarsely
        chopped honey-roasted
        peanuts

4 1/2 dozen cookies

Heat oven to 350°F (180°C). Lightly grease cookie sheets. Set aside. In large mixing bowl, combine sugars, butter, shortening, eggs and vanilla. Beat at medium speed of electric mixer until light and fluffy. Add flour, cornflakes, baking soda and salt. Beat at low speed until soft dough forms. Stir in peanut butter pieces and peanuts.

Drop dough by heaping teaspoons 2 inches (5 cm) apart onto prepared cookie sheets. Bake for 10 to 12 minutes, or until light golden brown. Cool completely before storing.

Chocolate Chip Cookies

Peppermint Chocolate Chip Drops

  2 *egg whites*
1/8 *teaspoon (0.5 mL) cream of tartar*
1/2 *cup (125 mL) sugar*
1/2 *cup (125 mL) miniature semisweet chocolate chips*
1/4 *cup (50 mL) finely crushed hard peppermint candies*

                  2 dozen cookies

Heat oven to 250°F (120°C). Line cookie sheets with parchment paper. Set aside. In medium mixing bowl, combine egg whites and cream of tartar. Beat at high speed of electric mixer until soft peaks begin to form. Add sugar, 1 tablespoon (15 mL) at a time, while beating at high speed. Beat until stiff peaks form. Fold in chips and candies.

Drop dough by rounded teaspoons 2 inches (5 cm) apart onto prepared cookie sheets. Bake for 25 to 30 minutes, or until dry. Cool completely before removing from parchment paper.

Tip: Egg whites should be at room temperature to produce greatest volume when beaten.

Chocolate Chip Cookies

Apricot Chip Cookies

1/2 cup (125 mL) granulated sugar
1/2 cup (125 mL) packed brown sugar
1/2 cup (125 mL) butter or margarine, softened
1 egg
1 teaspoon (5 mL) vanilla
1 1/4 cups (300 mL) all-purpose flour
1 cup (250 mL) uncooked old-fashioned rolled oats
1/2 cup (125 mL) flaked coconut
1/2 teaspoon (2 mL) baking soda
1/4 teaspoon (1 mL) salt
1/2 cup (125 mL) vanilla baking chips
1/2 cup (125 mL) coarsely chopped dried apricots
1/2 cup (125 mL) coarsely chopped macadamia nuts

About 3 dozen cookies

Heat oven to 375°F (190°C). In large mixing bowl, combine sugars, butter, egg and vanilla. Beat at medium speed of electric mixer until light and fluffy. Add flour, oats, coconut, baking soda and salt. Beat at low speed until soft dough forms. Stir in chips, apricots and nuts.

Drop dough by heaping teaspoons 2 inches (5 cm) apart onto ungreased cookie sheets. Bake for 7 to 10 minutes, or until edges are light golden brown. Let cool for 1 minute before removing from cookie sheets. Cool completely before storing.

Chocolate Chip Cookies

Chocolate Mint Cookies

1 cup (250 mL) butter or margarine, softened
3/4 cup (175 mL) packed brown sugar
1/2 cup (125 mL) granulated sugar
1 egg
1 teaspoon (5 mL) vanilla
2 cups (500 mL) all-purpose flour
1/4 cup (50 mL) unsweetened cocoa
1 teaspoon (5 mL) baking soda
1/2 teaspoon (2 mL) salt
1 pkg. (4.67 oz./132 g) chocolate sandwich mints, coarsely chopped
1 cup (250 mL) vanilla baking chips

Heat oven to 375°F (190°C). In large mixing bowl, combine butter, sugars, egg and vanilla. Beat at medium speed of electric mixer until light and fluffy. Add flour, cocoa, baking soda and salt. Beat at low speed until soft dough forms. Stir in mints and chips.

Drop dough by heaping teaspoons 2 inches (5 cm) apart onto ungreased cookie sheets. Bake for 8 to 10 minutes, or until set. Cool completely before storing.

3 dozen cookies

Chocolate Chip Cookies

Peanutty Sour Cream Cookies

- ½ cup (125 mL) granulated sugar
- ½ cup (125 mL) packed brown sugar
- ½ cup (125 mL) sour cream
- ¼ cup (50 mL) butter or margarine, softened
- ¼ cup (50 mL) vegetable shortening
- 1½ teaspoons (7 mL) vanilla
- 1¾ cups (425 mL) all-purpose flour
- ½ teaspoon (2 mL) baking soda
- ½ teaspoon (2 mL) salt
- 1 pkg. (8 oz./227g) candy-coated plain chocolate pieces
- 1 cup (250 mL) coarsely chopped peanuts

2½ dozen cookies

Heat oven to 375°F (190°C). In large mixing bowl, combine sugars, sour cream, butter, shortening and vanilla. Beat at medium speed of electric mixer until light and fluffy. Add flour, baking soda and salt. Beat at low speed until soft dough forms. Stir in chocolate pieces and peanuts.

Drop dough by heaping teaspoons 2 inches (5 cm) apart onto ungreased cookie sheets. Bake for 8 to 12 minutes, or until set. Cool completely before storing.

Chocolate Chip Cookies

Hawaiian Chocolate Chip Cookies

½ cup (125 mL) granulated sugar
½ cup (125 mL) packed brown sugar
½ cup (125 mL) butter or margarine, softened
1 egg
1 teaspoon (5 mL) vanilla
1½ cups (375 mL) all-purpose flour
½ cup (125 mL) flaked coconut
½ teaspoon (2 mL) baking soda
¼ teaspoon (1 mL) salt
1 cup (250 mL) semisweet chocolate chips
¾ cup (175 mL) coarsely chopped macadamia nuts

2½ dozen cookies

Heat oven to 375°F (190°C). In large mixing bowl, combine sugars, butter, egg and vanilla. Beat at medium speed of electric mixer until light and fluffy. Add flour, coconut, baking soda and salt. Beat at low speed until soft dough forms. Stir in chips and nuts.

Drop dough by heaping teaspoons 2 inches (5 cm) apart onto ungreased cookie sheets. Bake for 7 to 10 minutes, or until edges are light golden brown. Cool completely before storing.

Cranberry-Chip Cookies

½ cup (125 mL) sugar
½ cup (125 mL) vegetable shortening
2 eggs
1 teaspoon (5 mL) vanilla
1 cup (250 mL) all-purpose flour
1 cup (250 mL) uncooked quick-cooking oats
1 teaspoon (5 mL) baking powder
1 cup (250 mL) vanilla baking chips
½ cup (125 mL) dried cranberries
½ cup (125 mL) flaked coconut

3 dozen cookies

Heat oven to 350°F (180°C). In large mixing bowl, combine sugar, shortening, eggs and vanilla. Beat at medium speed of electric mixer until light and fluffy. Add flour, oats and baking powder. Beat at low speed until soft dough forms. Stir in chips, cranberries and coconut.

Drop dough by heaping teaspoons 2 inches (5 cm) apart onto ungreased cookie sheets. Bake for 9 to 11 minutes, or until set. Cool completely before storing.

Chocolate Chip Cookies

Triple Peanut Chocolate Chip Cookies

1 cup (250 mL) packed brown sugar
½ cup (125 mL) granulated sugar
½ cup (125 mL) butter or margarine, softened
½ cup (125 mL) vegetable shortening
½ cup (125 mL) creamy peanut butter
2 eggs
1 teaspoon (5 mL) vanilla
3 cups (750 mL) all-purpose flour
1 teaspoon (5 mL) baking soda
¼ teaspoon (1 mL) salt
½ cup (125 mL) peanut butter chips
½ cup (125 mL) semisweet chocolate chips
½ cup (125 mL) salted peanuts

3 dozen cookies

Heat oven to 350°F (180°C). In large mixing bowl, combine sugars, butter, shortening, peanut butter, eggs and vanilla. Beat at medium speed of electric mixer until well blended. Add flour, baking soda and salt. Beat at low speed until soft dough forms. Stir in chips and peanuts.

Drop dough by heaping teaspoons 2 inches (5 cm) apart onto ungreased cookie sheets. Bake for 10 to 12 minutes, or until light golden brown. Cool completely before storing.

Double Chocolate Peanut Butter Cookies

 1   cup (250 mL) packed brown
        sugar
 1/2 cup (125 mL) butter or
        margarine, softened
 1/2 cup (125 mL) vegetable
        shortening
 1/2 cup (125 mL) creamy
        peanut butter
 1   egg
 2   teaspoons (10 mL) vanilla
 2 1/2 cups (625 mL) uncooked
        old-fashioned rolled oats
 2   cups (500 mL) all-purpose
        flour
 1/4 teaspoon (1 mL) salt
 1/2 cup (125 mL) miniature
        semisweet chocolate chips
 36   miniature peanut butter cups

                3 dozen cookies

Heat oven to 350°F (180°C).
In large mixing bowl, combine
sugar, butter, shortening,
peanut butter, egg and vanilla.
Beat at medium speed of electric mixer until well blended.
Add oats, flour and salt. Beat
at low speed until soft dough
forms. Stir in chips.

Shape dough into 1 1/4-inch
(3 cm) balls. Place balls 2
inches (5 cm) apart on ungreased cookie sheets. Bake
for 10 to 14 minutes, or until
set. Immediately press peanut
butter cup into center of each
cookie. Let cool for 2 minutes before removing from
cookie sheets. Cool completely
before storing.

Cherry Vanilla Chip Cookies

 1 cup (250 mL) packed brown sugar
 6 squares (1 oz./30 g each) white baking
     chocolate, melted and slightly cooled
 3 eggs
1/2 cup (125 mL) vegetable shortening
1/4 cup (50 mL) butter or margarine, softened
1/4 cup (50 mL) granulated sugar
 3 cups (750 mL) all-purpose flour
 1 teaspoon (5 mL) baking soda
1/2 teaspoon (2 mL) salt
 1 cup (250 mL) vanilla baking chips
1/2 cup (125 mL) quartered maraschino cherries,
     well drained
1/2 cup (125 mL) coarsely chopped almonds

Heat oven to 350°F (180°C). In large mixing bowl, combine brown sugar, melted white chocolate, eggs, shortening, butter and granulated sugar. Beat at medium speed of electric mixer until well blended. Add flour, baking soda and salt. Beat at low speed until soft dough forms. Stir in chips, cherries and almonds.

Drop dough by heaping teaspoons 2 inches (5 cm) apart onto ungreased cookie sheets. Bake for 8 to 12 minutes, or until light golden brown. Let cool for 1 minute before removing from cookie sheets. Cool completely before storing.

3 dozen cookies

Chocolate Chip Cookies

Crunchy Butterscotch Chip Cookies

  1 *cup (250 mL) packed brown sugar*
  3/4 *cup (175 mL) butterscotch chips, melted and*
     slightly cooled
  3 *eggs*
  1/2 *cup (125 mL) vegetable shortening*
  1/4 *cup (50 mL) butter or margarine, softened*
  1/4 *cup (50 mL) granulated sugar*
3 1/4 *cups (800 mL) all-purpose flour*
  1 *cup (250 mL) crushed whole-grain wheat flakes*
  1 *teaspoon (5 mL) baking soda*
  1/2 *teaspoon (2 mL) salt*
  1/2 *cup (125 mL) semisweet chocolate chips*
  1/2 *cup (125 mL) chopped cashews*

About 2 1/2 dozen cookies

Heat oven to 350°F (180°C). In large mixing bowl, combine brown sugar, melted butterscotch chips, eggs, shortening, butter and granulated sugar. Beat at medium speed of electric mixer until well blended. Add flour, wheat flakes, baking soda and salt. Beat at low speed until soft dough forms. Stir in chocolate chips and cashews.

Drop dough by heaping teaspoons 2 inches (5 cm) apart onto ungreased cookie sheets. Bake for 8 to 12 minutes, or until light golden brown. Let cool for 1 minute before removing from cookie sheets. Cool completely before storing.

Oats 'n Yogurt Chip Cookies

1/2 cup (125 mL) plain nonfat or low-fat yogurt
1/2 cup (125 mL) granulated sugar
1/2 cup (125 mL) packed brown sugar
1/4 cup (50 mL) butter or margarine, softened
1/4 cup (50 mL) vegetable shortening
1 teaspoon (5 mL) vanilla
1 3/4 cups (425 mL) all-purpose flour
1/2 cup (125 mL) uncooked old-fashioned rolled oats
1/2 teaspoon (2 mL) baking soda
1/4 teaspoon (1 mL) salt
1/2 cup (125 mL) semisweet chocolate chips
1/2 cup (125 mL) milk chocolate chips

About 3 dozen cookies

Heat oven to 375°F (190°C). In large mixing bowl, combine yogurt, sugars, butter, shortening and vanilla. Beat at medium speed of electric mixer until well blended. Add flour, oats, baking soda and salt. Beat at low speed until soft dough forms. Stir in chips.

Drop dough by heaping teaspoons 2 inches (5 cm) apart onto ungreased cookie sheets. Bake for 8 to 12 minutes, or until light golden brown. Let cool for 1 minute before removing from cookie sheets. Cool completely before storing.

Triple Chocolate Chip Cookies

1¼ cups (300 mL) packed
     brown sugar
  3 eggs
½ cup (125 mL) vegetable
     shortening
¼ cup (50 mL) butter or
     margarine, softened
  4 squares (1 oz./30g each)
     semisweet baking chocolate,
     melted and slightly cooled
  2 teaspoons (10 mL) vanilla
  3 cups (750 mL) all-purpose
     flour
  1 teaspoon (5 mL) baking soda
¼ teaspoon (1 mL) salt
  4 squares (1 oz./30 g each)
     white baking chocolate,
     coarsely chopped
  1 cup (250 mL) semisweet
     chocolate chips
  1 cup (250 mL) milk chocolate
     chips
  1 cup (250 mL) chopped
     pecans

About 3 dozen cookies

Heat oven to 375°F (190°C). In
large mixing bowl, combine
sugar, eggs, shortening, butter,
melted semisweet chocolate
and vanilla. Beat at medium
speed of electric mixer until
well blended. Add flour, baking soda and salt. Beat at low
speed until soft dough forms.
Stir in white chocolate, chips
and pecans.

Drop dough by heaping teaspoons 2 inches (5 cm) apart
onto ungreased cookie sheets.
Bake for 9 to 11 minutes, or
until set. Let cool for 2 minutes before removing from
cookie sheets. Cool completely
before storing.

Chocolate Chip Cookies

Giant Potato Chip Cookies

1 cup (250 mL) granulated
   sugar
1 cup (250 mL) packed brown
   sugar
1 cup (250 mL) vegetable
   shortening
2 eggs
2 teaspoons (10 mL) vanilla
2 cups (500 mL) all-purpose
   flour
1 cup (250 mL) uncooked
   old-fashioned rolled oats
1/2 cup (125 mL) crushed
   potato chips
1 teaspoon (5 mL) baking
   powder
1 teaspoon (5 mL) baking soda
1 cup (250 mL) miniature
   candy-coated semisweet
   chocolate pieces
1/2 cup (125 mL) chopped
   mixed nuts

2 dozen cookies

Heat oven to 350°F (180°C). In
large mixing bowl, combine
sugars, shortening, eggs and
vanilla. Beat at medium speed
of electric mixer until light and
fluffy. Add flour, oats, potato
chips, baking powder and baking soda. Beat at low speed
until soft dough forms. Stir in
chocolate pieces and nuts.

Drop dough by 1/4 cups (50 mL)
3 inches (8 cm) apart onto ungreased cookie sheets. Bake
for 13 to 16 minutes, or until
golden brown. Let cool for 2
minutes before removing from
cookie sheets. Cool completely
before storing.

Sunflower-Chip Cookies

1 cup (250 mL) granulated sugar
1 cup (250 mL) packed brown sugar
1/2 cup (125 mL) butter or margarine, softened
1/2 cup (125 mL) vegetable shortening
2 eggs
1 1/2 teaspoons (7 mL) vanilla
2 cups (500 mL) all-purpose flour
1 cup (250 mL) uncooked old-fashioned rolled oats
1/2 cup (125 mL) whole-grain wheat flakes
1/2 cup (125 mL) flaked coconut
1 teaspoon (5 mL) baking powder
1 teaspoon (5 mL) baking soda
1/4 teaspoon (1 mL) salt
1/2 cup (125 mL) semisweet chocolate chips
1/2 cup (125 mL) vanilla baking chips
1/2 cup (125 mL) shelled sunflower seeds

1 1/2 dozen cookies

Heat oven to 350°F (180°C). In large mixing bowl, combine sugars, butter, shortening, eggs and vanilla. Beat at medium speed of electric mixer until light and fluffy. Add flour, oats, wheat flakes, coconut, baking powder, baking soda and salt. Beat at low speed until soft dough forms. Stir in chips and seeds.

Drop dough by 1/4 cups (50 mL) 3 inches (8 cm) apart onto ungreased cookie sheets. Flatten dough slightly with back of spoon. Bake for 13 to 16 minutes, or until golden brown. Let cool for 2 minutes before removing from cookie sheets. Cool completely before storing.

Chocolate Chip Cookies

Candied Orange 'n Chip Cookies

1 cup (250 mL) granulated sugar
1 cup (250 mL) packed brown sugar
1/2 cup (125 mL) butter or margarine, softened
1/2 cup (125 mL) vegetable shortening
2 eggs
1 teaspoon (5 mL) vanilla
2 cups (500 mL) all-purpose flour
2 cups (500 mL) uncooked old-fashioned rolled oats
1 cup (250 mL) flaked coconut
1/4 teaspoon (1 mL) salt
1 cup (250 mL) chopped orange slice candies
1 cup (250 mL) milk chocolate chips
1/2 cup (125 mL) chopped pecans

About 4 dozen cookies

Heat oven to 350°F (180°C). Lightly grease cookie sheets. Set aside. In large mixing bowl, combine sugars, butter, shortening, eggs and vanilla. Beat at medium speed of electric mixer until light and fluffy. Add flour, oats, coconut and salt. Beat at low speed until soft dough forms. Stir in candies, chips and pecans.

Drop dough by heaping teaspoons 2 inches (5 cm) apart onto prepared cookie sheets. Bake for 13 to 16 minutes, or until edges are golden brown. Cool completely before storing.

Chocolate Chip Cookies

Butterscotch Chocolate Chip Cookies

1 cup (250 mL) granulated sugar
1 cup (250 mL) packed brown sugar
1/2 cup (125 mL) butter or margarine, softened
1/2 cup (125 mL) vegetable shortening
2 eggs
1 teaspoon (5 mL) vanilla
2 cups (500 mL) all-purpose flour
2 cups (500 mL) uncooked old-fashioned rolled oats
1 teaspoon (5 mL) baking soda
1/2 teaspoon (2 mL) baking powder
1/4 teaspoon (1 mL) salt
1/2 cup (125 mL) butterscotch chips
1/2 cup (125 mL) semisweet chocolate chips
1/2 cup (125 mL) chopped walnuts

Heat oven to 350°F (180°C). In large mixing bowl, combine sugars, butter, shortening, eggs and vanilla. Beat at medium speed of electric mixer until light and fluffy. Add flour, oats, baking soda, baking powder and salt. Beat at low speed until soft dough forms. Stir in chips and walnuts.

Drop dough by heaping teaspoons 2 inches (5 cm) apart onto ungreased cookie sheets. Bake for 10 to 12 minutes, or until light golden brown. Cool completely before storing.

About 4 dozen cookies

Chocolate Chip Cookies

Almond Toffee Bit Cookies

½   cup (125 mL) granulated
      sugar
½   cup (125 mL) packed brown
      sugar
½   cup (125 mL) butter or
      margarine, softened
1   egg
1   teaspoon (5 mL) almond extract
1¼ cups (300 mL) all-purpose
      flour
1   cup (250 mL) uncooked
      old-fashioned rolled oats
½   teaspoon (2 mL) baking soda
¼   teaspoon (1 mL) salt
1   cup (250 mL) semisweet
      chocolate chips
¾   cup (175 mL) English
      toffee bits

About 2 dozen cookies

Heat oven to 350°F (180°C).
Lightly grease cookie sheets.
Set aside. In large mixing bowl,
combine sugars, butter, egg and
almond extract. Beat at medium
speed of electric mixer until
light and fluffy. Add flour, oats,
baking soda and salt. Beat at
low speed until soft dough
forms. Stir in bits.

Drop dough by heaping teaspoons 2 inches (5 cm) apart
onto prepared cookie sheets.
Bake for 8 to 10 minutes, or until
light golden brown. Let cool for
1 minute before removing from
cookie sheets. Cool completely
before storing.

Chocolate Chip Cookies

Chocolate Chip Granola Cookies

1¼ cups (300 mL) packed
    brown sugar
¾ cup (175 mL) vegetable
    shortening
½ cup (125 mL) granulated
    sugar
¼ cup (50 mL) butter or
    margarine, softened
2 eggs
2 tablespoons (25 mL) milk
2 teaspoons (10 mL) vanilla
3 cups (750 mL) granola
2½ cups (625 mL) all-purpose
    flour
1 teaspoon (5 mL) baking soda
½ teaspoon (2 mL) salt
1 cup (250 mL) semisweet
    chocolate chips
1 cup (250 mL) milk chocolate
    chips

About 4½ dozen cookies

Heat oven to 350°F (180°C).
In large mixing bowl, combine
brown sugar, shortening, granulated sugar, butter, eggs, milk
and vanilla. Beat at medium
speed of electric mixer until
light and fluffy. Add granola,
flour, baking soda and salt.
Beat at low speed until soft
dough forms. Stir in chips.

Drop dough by heaping teaspoons 2 inches (5 cm) apart
onto ungreased cookie sheets.
Bake for 10 to 12 minutes, or
until light golden brown. Cool
completely before storing.

Chocolate Chip Cookies

Rainbow Oat S'mores

   1 cup (250 mL) packed brown sugar
 1/2 cup (125 mL) granulated sugar
 1/2 cup (125 mL) butter or margarine, softened
 1/2 cup (125 mL) vegetable shortening
   2 eggs
1 1/2 teaspoons (7 mL) vanilla
   3 cups (750 mL) all-purpose flour
1 1/2 cups (375 mL) uncooked old-fashioned rolled oats
   1 teaspoon (5 mL) baking soda
 1/4 teaspoon (1 mL) salt
   1 cup (250 mL) rainbow semisweet chocolate
      chips
   1 cup (250 mL) miniature marshmallows

5 dozen cookies

Heat oven to 350°F (180°C). Lightly grease cookie sheets. Set aside. In large mixing bowl, combine sugars, butter, shortening, eggs and vanilla. Beat at medium speed of electric mixer until well blended. Add flour, oats, baking soda and salt. Beat at low speed until soft dough forms. Stir in chips and marshmallows.

Drop dough by heaping teaspoons 2 inches (5 cm) apart onto prepared cookie sheets. Bake for 10 to 13 minutes, or until light golden brown. Let cool for 1 minute before removing from cookie sheets. Cool completely before storing.

Chocolate Raisin Oat Cookies

1 cup (250 mL) granulated sugar
1 cup (250 mL) packed brown sugar
1 cup (250 mL) butter or margarine, softened
2 eggs
2 teaspoons (10 mL) vanilla
3 cups (750 mL) uncooked old-fashioned rolled oats
2 cups (500 mL) all-purpose flour
1 teaspoon (5 mL) baking powder
1/2 teaspoon (2 mL) baking soda
1/2 teaspoon (2 mL) salt
1 cup (250 mL) chocolate-covered raisins
1 cup (250 mL) chopped pecans

4 dozen cookies

Heat oven to 350°F (180°C). Lightly grease cookie sheets. Set aside. In large mixing bowl, combine sugars, butter, eggs and vanilla. Beat at medium speed of electric mixer until light and fluffy. Add oats, flour, baking powder, baking soda and salt. Beat at low speed until soft dough forms. Stir in raisins and pecans.

Drop dough by heaping teaspoons 2 inches (5 cm) apart onto prepared cookie sheets. Bake for 12 to 15 minutes, or until edges are golden brown. Let cool for 1 minute before removing from cookie sheets. Cool completely before storing.

Chocolate Chip Cookies

Banana Chocolate Nut Drops

1 cup (250 mL) mashed
   bananas (2 medium)
1 cup (250 mL) sugar
1/2 cup (125 mL) butter or
   margarine, softened
1/4 cup (50 mL) vegetable
   shortening
1 egg
1/2 teaspoon (2 mL) vanilla
2 cups (500 mL) all-purpose
   flour
1/2 cup (125 mL) unsweetened
   cocoa
1 teaspoon (5 mL) baking soda
1/4 teaspoon (1 mL) salt
3/4 cup (175 mL) coarsely
   chopped macadamia nuts
1/2 cup (125 mL) miniature
   semisweet chocolate chips

2 1/2 dozen cookies

Heat oven to 350°F (180°C).
Lightly grease cookie sheets.
Set aside. In large mixing bowl,
combine bananas, sugar, butter, shortening, egg and vanilla. Beat at medium speed of
electric mixer until well blended.
Add flour, cocoa, baking soda
and salt. Beat at low speed
until soft dough forms. Stir
in nuts and chips.

Drop dough by heaping teaspoons 2 inches (5 cm) apart
onto prepared cookie sheets.
Bake for 12 to 14 minutes, or
until set. Let cool for 2 minutes
before removing from cookie
sheets. Cool completely before
storing.

Chunky Macadamia Chip Cookies

   1 cup (250 mL) packed brown
     sugar
 1/2 cup (125 mL) granulated
     sugar
 1/2 cup (125 mL) butter or
     margarine, softened
 1/2 cup (125 mL) vegetable
     shortening
   2 eggs
1 1/2 teaspoons (7 mL) vanilla
   3 cups (750 mL) all-purpose
     flour
   1 cup (250 mL) flaked coconut
   1 teaspoon (5 mL) baking soda
 1/4 teaspoon (1 mL) salt
 3/4 cup (175 mL) coarsely
     chopped macadamia nuts
 1/2 cup (125 mL) chopped white
     baking chocolate or vanilla
     baking chips
 1/2 cup (125 mL) milk chocolate
     chips

5 dozen cookies

Heat oven to 350°F (180°C). In
large mixing bowl, combine
sugars, butter, shortening, eggs
and vanilla. Beat at medium
speed of electric mixer until
light and fluffy. Add flour,
coconut, baking soda and salt.
Beat at low speed until soft
dough forms. Stir in nuts,
white chocolate and chips.

Drop dough by heaping teaspoons 2 inches (5 cm) apart
onto ungreased cookie sheets.
Bake for 11 to 13 minutes, or
until light golden brown. Let
cool for 1 minute before removing from cookie sheets. Cool
completely before storing.

Hearty Cookies

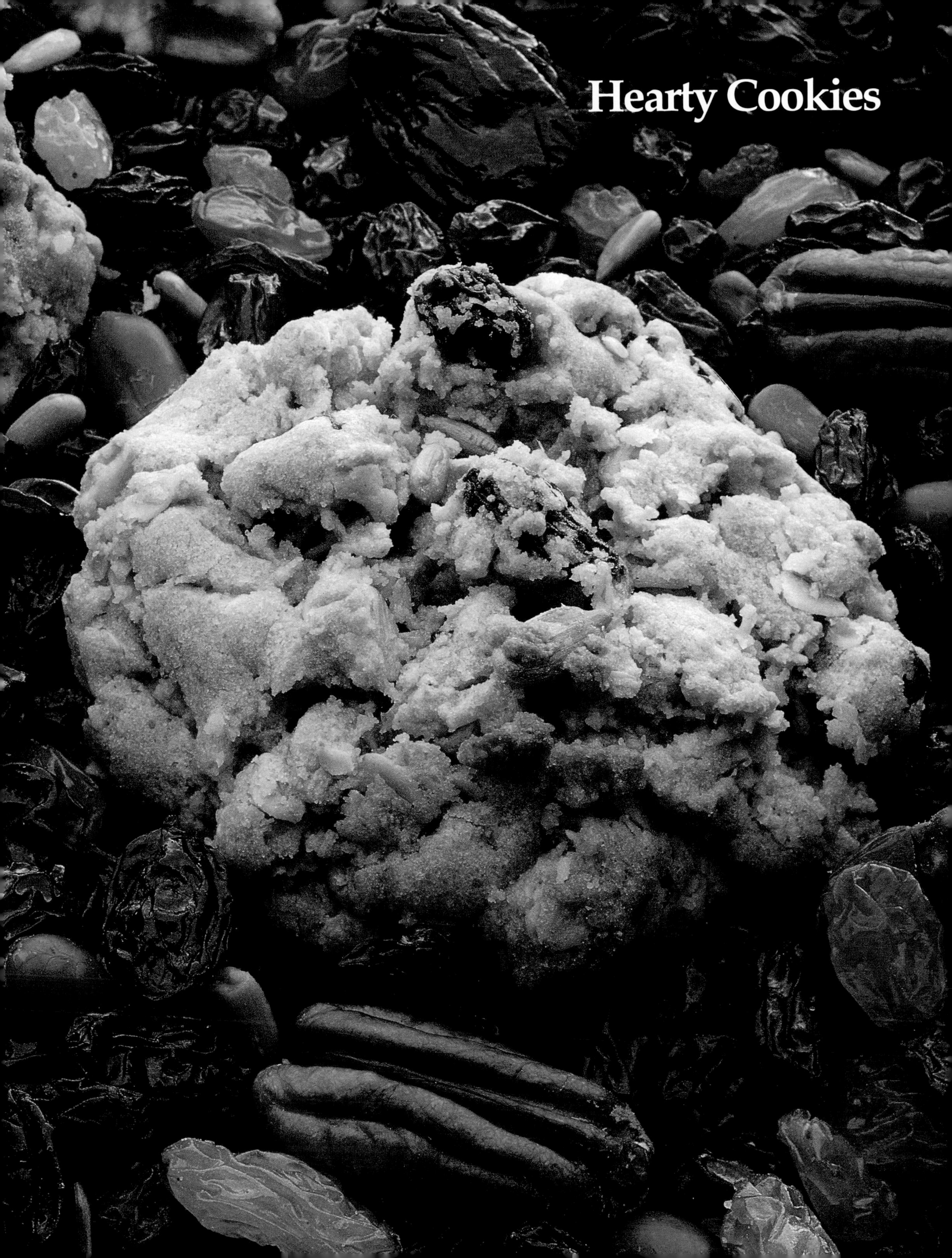

Oats

Hearty Cookie Basics

Hearty cookies are full of wholesome, nutritious ingredients. They have generous helpings of oats, dried fruits, nuts, peanut butter, coconut, cereals and even fresh fruits and vegetables. They are a high-energy food and are filling for hearty appetites. Take these cookies hiking or camping, serve them as an after-school snack or eat them any time a quick energy boost is needed.

Honey

Flaked
coconut

Dried fruits

Most of the recipes in this chapter are prepared like drop cookies, so they are quick and easy to make. Because of the hearty ingredients added, be particularly careful to follow the doneness tests indicated in the recipes.

Hearty cookies freeze well, and thawing takes just a short time at room temperature. Wrap the cookies individually in plastic wrap, then foil, for trips or lunches — the cookies will stay fresh and the foil will help keep them from being crushed. Or pack cookies while they are still frozen and allow them to thaw while being toted.

Nuts

Flaked cereal

Peanut butter

Granola

Peanut Butter Trail Mix Cookies

2 cups (500 mL) uncooked
  old-fashioned rolled oats
1/2 cup (125 mL) packed brown
  sugar
1/2 cup (125 mL) butter or
  margarine, softened
1/2 cup (125 mL) chunky
  peanut butter
1 1/2 teaspoons (7 mL) vanilla
3/4 cup (175 mL) all-purpose
  flour
1/2 cup (125 mL) mashed
  banana (1 medium)
1 1/2 teaspoons (7 mL) baking
  powder
1/2 teaspoon (2 mL) salt
1 cup (250 mL) trail mix

About 3 dozen cookies

Heat oven to 350°F (180°C). In food processor or blender, process oats until coarsely ground. Set aside.

In large mixing bowl, combine sugar, butter, peanut butter and vanilla. Beat at medium speed of electric mixer until light and fluffy. Add oats, flour, banana, baking powder and salt. Beat at low speed until soft dough forms. Stir in trail mix.

Drop dough by heaping teaspoons 2 inches (5 cm) apart onto ungreased cookie sheets. Bake for 8 to 10 minutes, or until set. Cool completely before storing.

Carrot Bran Cookies

1/2 cup (125 mL) sugar
1/2 cup (125 mL) vegetable
    shortening
1 egg
1 teaspoon (5 mL) vanilla
1 cup (250 mL) whole wheat
    flour
1 cup (250 mL) bran flakes
1/2 teaspoon (2 mL) ground
    cinnamon
1/2 teaspoon (2 mL) baking soda
1/4 teaspoon (1 mL) baking
    powder
1/4 teaspoon (1 mL) salt
1/2 cup (125 mL) grated carrot
1/2 cup (125 mL) raisins

About 2 1/2 dozen cookies

Heat oven to 350°F (180°C). In large mixing bowl, combine sugar, shortening, egg and vanilla. Beat at medium speed of electric mixer until well blended. Add flour, bran flakes, cinnamon, baking soda, baking powder and salt. Beat at low speed until soft dough forms. Stir in carrot and raisins.

Shape dough into 1-inch (2.5 cm) balls. Place balls 2 inches (5 cm) apart on un-greased cookie sheets. Bake for 8 to 10 minutes, or until set. Let cool for 1 minute before removing from cookie sheets. Cool completely before storing.

Breakfast Prune Cookies

½ cup (125 mL) packed brown
   sugar
½ cup (125 mL) vegetable
   shortening
¼ cup (50 mL) butter or
   margarine, softened
1 egg
1 teaspoon (5 mL) vanilla
2 cups (500 mL) uncooked
   quick-cooking oats
1 cup (250 mL) whole wheat
   flour
½ teaspoon (2 mL) baking soda
½ teaspoon (2 mL) ground
   cinnamon
¼ teaspoon (1 mL) ground
   ginger
¼ teaspoon (1 mL) ground
   cloves
¼ teaspoon (1 mL) salt
1 cup (250 mL) chopped
   orange essence prunes
1 cup (250 mL) finely chopped
   cooking apple
1 cup (250 mL) chopped pecans

3 dozen cookies

Heat oven to 350°F (180°C).
Lightly grease cookie sheets.
Set aside. In large mixing
bowl, combine sugar, shortening, butter, egg and vanilla.
Beat at medium speed of electric mixer until light and fluffy.
Add oats, flour, baking soda,
cinnamon, ginger, cloves and
salt. Beat at low speed until
soft dough forms. Stir in
prunes, apple and pecans.

Drop dough by heaping teaspoons 2 inches (5 cm) apart
onto prepared cookie sheets.
Bake for 8 to 12 minutes, or
until golden brown. Cool completely before storing.

Zucchini Raisin Cookies

1 cup (250 mL) packed brown sugar
1 cup (250 mL) butter or margarine, softened
1 egg
1 teaspoon (5 mL) vanilla
1 teaspoon (5 mL) grated orange peel
2¹/₂ cups (625 mL) crushed whole-grain wheat flakes
1¹/₂ cups (375 mL) all-purpose flour
¹/₂ cup (125 mL) wheat germ
¹/₂ teaspoon (2 mL) baking soda
¹/₂ teaspoon (2 mL) ground allspice
³/₄ cup (175 mL) grated zucchini
¹/₂ cup (125 mL) golden raisins

Heat oven to 375°F (190°C). In large mixing bowl, combine sugar, butter, egg, vanilla and peel. Beat at medium speed of electric mixer until light and fluffy. Add wheat flakes, flour, wheat germ, baking soda and allspice. Beat at low speed until soft dough forms. Stir in zucchini and raisins.

Drop dough by heaping teaspoons 2 inches (5 cm) apart onto ungreased cookie sheets. Bake for 9 to 12 minutes, or until golden brown. Let cool for 1 minute before removing from cookie sheets. Cool completely before storing.

About 3 dozen cookies

Hearty Cookies

Apricot Pine Nut Cookies

1/2 cup (125 mL) pine nuts
3/4 cup (175 mL) packed brown sugar
1/2 cup (125 mL) butter or margarine, softened
1 egg
1 teaspoon (5 mL) vanilla
2 cups (500 mL) crisp oatmeal flakes
1 cup (250 mL) all-purpose flour
1/3 cup (75 mL) flaked coconut
1/2 teaspoon (2 mL) baking soda
1/4 teaspoon (1 mL) salt
1/2 cup (125 mL) chopped dried apricots

About 2 1/2 dozen cookies

Heat oven to 400°F (200°C). Lightly grease cookie sheets. Set aside. Place pine nuts in 8-inch (2 L) square baking pan. Bake for 4 to 5 minutes, or until golden brown, stirring twice. Set aside. Reduce oven temperature to 350°F (180°C).

In large mixing bowl, combine sugar, butter, egg and vanilla. Beat at medium speed of electric mixer until light and fluffy. Add oatmeal flakes, flour, coconut, baking soda and salt. Beat at low speed until soft dough forms. Stir in pine nuts and apricots.

Drop dough by heaping teaspoons 2 inches (5 cm) apart onto prepared cookie sheets. Bake for 5 to 7 minutes, or until light golden brown. Let cool for 1 minute before removing from cookie sheets. Cool completely before storing.

Hearty Cookies

Apple Crunch Cookies

½ cup (125 mL) sugar
½ cup (125 mL) vegetable shortening
1 egg
1 teaspoon (5 mL) vanilla
1½ cups (375 mL) bran flakes
1 cup (250 mL) all-purpose flour
½ teaspoon (2 mL) baking soda
1 cup (250 mL) finely chopped peeled
    cooking apple
½ cup (125 mL) chopped dried apricots
⅓ cup (75 mL) chopped pecans

About 2½ dozen cookies

Heat oven to 350°F (180°C). In large mixing bowl, combine sugar, shortening, egg and vanilla. Beat at medium speed of electric mixer until well blended. Add bran flakes, flour and baking soda. Beat at low speed until soft dough forms. Stir in apple, apricots and pecans.

Drop dough by heaping teaspoons 2 inches (5 cm) apart onto ungreased cookie sheets. Bake for 10 to 12 minutes, or until light golden brown. Let cool for 1 minute before removing from cookie sheets. Cool completely before storing.

Yogurt Granola Cookies

1/2 cup (125 mL) plain nonfat
   or low-fat yogurt
1/2 cup (125 mL) granulated
   sugar
1/2 cup (125 mL) packed brown
   sugar
1/4 cup (50 mL) butter or
   margarine, softened
1/4 cup (50 mL) vegetable
   shortening
2 teaspoons (10 mL) vanilla
1 3/4 cups (425 mL) all-purpose
   flour
1/2 teaspoon (2 mL) baking soda
1/2 teaspoon (2 mL) salt
2 cups (500 mL) granola
1/2 cup (125 mL) miniature
   candy-coated semisweet
   chocolate chips
1/2 cup (125 mL) flaked coconut
1/2 cup (125 mL) coarsely
   chopped walnuts

3 dozen cookies

Heat oven to 375°F (190°C). In large mixing bowl, combine yogurt, sugars, butter, shortening and vanilla. Beat at medium speed of electric mixer until well blended. Add flour, baking soda and salt. Beat at low speed until soft dough forms. Stir in granola, chips, coconut and walnuts.

Drop dough by heaping teaspoons 2 inches (5 cm) apart onto ungreased cookie sheets. Bake for 8 to 10 minutes, or until set. Let cool for 1 minute before removing from cookie sheets. Cool completely before storing.

Granola Date Cookies

2 cups (500 mL) packed
    brown sugar
1/2 cup (125 mL) butter or
    margarine, softened
1/2 cup (125 mL) vegetable
    shortening
2 eggs
1 teaspoon (5 mL) vanilla
2 cups (500 mL) granola
1 cup (250 mL) all-purpose
    flour
1 cup (250 mL) whole wheat
    flour
1/2 teaspoon (2 mL) baking
    powder
1/2 teaspoon (2 mL) baking
    soda
1/2 teaspoon (2 mL) ground
    cinnamon
1/4 teaspoon (1 mL) salt
1 cup (250 mL) chopped dates

3 1/2 dozen cookies

Heat oven to 350°F (180°C)
Lightly grease cookie sheets.
Set aside. In large mixing bowl,
combine sugar, butter, shortening, eggs and vanilla. Beat at
medium speed of electric mixer
until light and fluffy. Add
granola, flours, baking powder, baking soda, cinnamon
and salt. Beat at low speed
until soft dough forms. Stir
in dates.

Drop dough by heaping teaspoons 2 inches (5 cm) apart
onto prepared cookie sheets.
Bake for 8 to 12 minutes, or
until golden brown. Let cool
for 1 minute before removing
from cookie sheets. Cool completely before storing.

Hearty Cookies

Hearty Peanut Butter Raisin Cookies

2 cups (500 mL) packed brown sugar
1 cup (250 mL) creamy peanut butter
1/2 cup (125 mL) butter or margarine, softened
1/2 cup (125 mL) vegetable shortening
2 eggs
2 teaspoons (10 mL) vanilla
2 cups (500 mL) uncooked old-fashioned rolled oats
1 3/4 cups (425 mL) all-purpose flour
1/2 cup (125 mL) whole wheat flour
1 teaspoon (5 mL) baking soda
1/2 teaspoon (2 mL) baking powder
1/2 teaspoon (2 mL) salt
1 cup (250 mL) raisins
1/2 cup (125 mL) shelled sunflower seeds

4 1/2 dozen cookies

Heat oven to 350°F (180°C). In large mixing bowl, combine sugar, peanut butter, butter, shortening, eggs and vanilla. Beat at medium speed of electric mixer until well blended. Add oats, flours, baking soda, baking powder and salt. Beat at low speed until soft dough forms. Stir in raisins and seeds.

Drop dough by heaping teaspoons 2 inches (5 cm) apart onto ungreased cookie sheets. Bake for 10 to 12 minutes, or until golden brown. Let cool for 1 minute before removing from cookie sheets. Cool completely before storing.

Hearty Cookies

Applesauce Date Cookies

  1 *cup (250 mL) unsweetened applesauce*
1/2 *cup (125 mL) granulated sugar*
1/2 *cup (125 mL) packed brown sugar*
1/2 *cup (125 mL) vegetable shortening*
  1 *egg*
2 1/2 *cups (625 mL) all-purpose flour*
  1 *cup (250 mL) uncooked quick-cooking oats*
  1 *teaspoon (5 mL) baking soda*
1/2 *teaspoon (2 mL) baking powder*
1/2 *teaspoon (2 mL) ground cinnamon*
1/4 *teaspoon (1 mL) ground cloves*
1/4 *teaspoon (1 mL) salt*
1/2 *cup (125 mL) chopped dates*

About 3 1/2 dozen cookies

Heat oven to 375°F (190°C). Lightly grease cookie sheets. Set aside. In large mixing bowl, combine applesauce, sugars, shortening and egg. Beat at medium speed of electric mixer until well blended. Add flour, oats, baking soda, baking powder, cinnamon, cloves and salt. Beat at low speed until soft dough forms. Stir in dates.

Drop dough by heaping teaspoons 2 inches (5 cm) apart onto prepared cookie sheets. Bake for 8 to 10 minutes, or until light golden brown. Let cool for 1 minute before removing from cookie sheets. Cool completely before storing.

Crunchy Chocolate Chip Cookies

1/2 *cup (125 mL) butter or margarine, softened*
1/2 *cup (125 mL) packed brown sugar*
1/4 *cup (50 mL) granulated sugar*
1/4 *cup (50 mL) frozen cholesterol-free egg product, defrosted, or 1 egg*
1 1/2 *teaspoons (7 mL) vanilla*
1 *cup (250 mL) all-purpose flour*
1 1/4 *cups (300 mL) uncooked quick-cooking oats*
1/2 *cup (125 mL) cornflakes*
1/2 *teaspoon (2 mL) baking soda*
1/4 *teaspoon (1 mL) salt*
1/2 *cup (125 mL) semisweet chocolate chips*
1/4 *cup (50 mL) shelled sunflower seeds*

About 2 1/2 dozen cookies

Heat oven to 350°F (180°C). Lightly grease cookie sheets. Set aside. In large mixing bowl, combine butter, sugars, egg product and vanilla. Beat at medium speed of electric mixer until well blended. Add flour, oats, cornflakes, baking soda and salt. Beat at low speed until soft dough forms. Stir in chips and seeds.

Drop dough by heaping teaspoons 2 inches (5 cm) apart onto prepared cookie sheets. Bake for 8 to 10 minutes, or until light golden brown. Cool completely before storing.

Molasses Prune Cookies

3/4 cup (175 mL) pitted prunes
1/3 cup (75 mL) hot water
3/4 cup (175 mL) packed brown sugar
1/4 cup (50 mL) granulated sugar
1/4 cup (50 mL) light molasses
1 egg
2 1/4 cups (550 mL) all-purpose flour
1 1/4 cups (300 mL) uncooked old-fashioned rolled oats
1 teaspoon (5 mL) ground cinnamon
1/2 teaspoon (2 mL) baking soda
1/2 teaspoon (2 mL) ground cloves
1/4 teaspoon (1 mL) ground ginger
1/4 teaspoon (1 mL) salt
Granulated sugar

3 1/2 dozen cookies

In food processor or blender, combine prunes and water. Process until smooth. In large mixing bowl, combine prune mixture, brown sugar, 1/4 cup (50 mL) granulated sugar, the molasses and egg. Beat at medium speed of electric mixer until well blended. Add flour, oats, cinnamon, baking soda, cloves, ginger and salt. Beat at low speed until soft dough forms. Cover with plastic wrap. Chill 2 to 3 hours, or until dough is easy to handle.

Heat oven to 350°F (180°C). Lightly grease cookie sheets. Set aside. Roll dough into 1-inch (2.5 cm) balls. (Lightly flour hands to prevent dough from sticking.) Roll balls in granulated sugar. Place balls 2 inches (5 cm) apart on prepared cookie sheets. Bake for 8 to 12 minutes, or until set. Let cool for 1 minute before removing from cookie sheets. Cool completely before storing.

Hearty Cookies

Sunny Peach Cookies

1 cup (250 mL) packed brown sugar
1 cup (250 mL) butter or margarine, softened
1/2 cup (125 mL) honey
2 eggs
2 teaspoons (10 mL) vanilla
1 3/4 cups (425 mL) all-purpose flour
1 teaspoon (5 mL) baking soda
1/2 teaspoon (2 mL) salt
2 1/2 cups (625 mL) uncooked old-fashioned rolled oats
1 pkg. (7 oz./198 g) dried peaches, chopped
1/2 cup (125 mL) shelled sunflower seeds

4 1/2 dozen cookies

Heat oven to 350°F (180°C). Lightly grease cookie sheets. Set aside. In large mixing bowl, combine sugar, butter, honey, eggs and vanilla. Beat at medium speed of electric mixer until well blended. Add flour, baking soda and salt. Beat at low speed until soft dough forms. Stir in oats, peaches and seeds.

Drop dough by heaping teaspoons 2 inches (5 cm) apart onto prepared cookie sheets. Bake for 9 to 10 minutes, or until edges are golden brown. Cool completely before storing.

Tip: Dried apricots can be substituted for dried peaches.

Banana Walnut Cookies

1 cup (250 mL) packed brown sugar
3/4 cup (175 mL) butter or margarine, softened
1/2 cup (125 mL) granulated sugar
1 teaspoon (5 mL) vanilla
2 cups (500 mL) all-purpose flour
1 cup (250 mL) buttermilk
3/4 cup (175 mL) mashed bananas (2 small)
1 teaspoon (5 mL) baking soda
1/2 teaspoon (2 mL) salt
2 1/2 cups (625 mL) uncooked old-fashioned rolled oats
3/4 cup (175 mL) chopped walnuts

4 dozen cookies

Heat oven to 350°F (180°C). In large mixing bowl, combine brown sugar, butter, granulated sugar and vanilla. Beat at medium speed of electric mixer until light and fluffy. Add flour, buttermilk, bananas, baking soda and salt. Beat at low speed until soft dough forms. Stir in oats and walnuts.

Drop dough by heaping teaspoons 2 inches (5 cm) apart onto ungreased cookie sheets. Bake for 9 to 10 minutes, or until golden brown. Cool completely before storing.

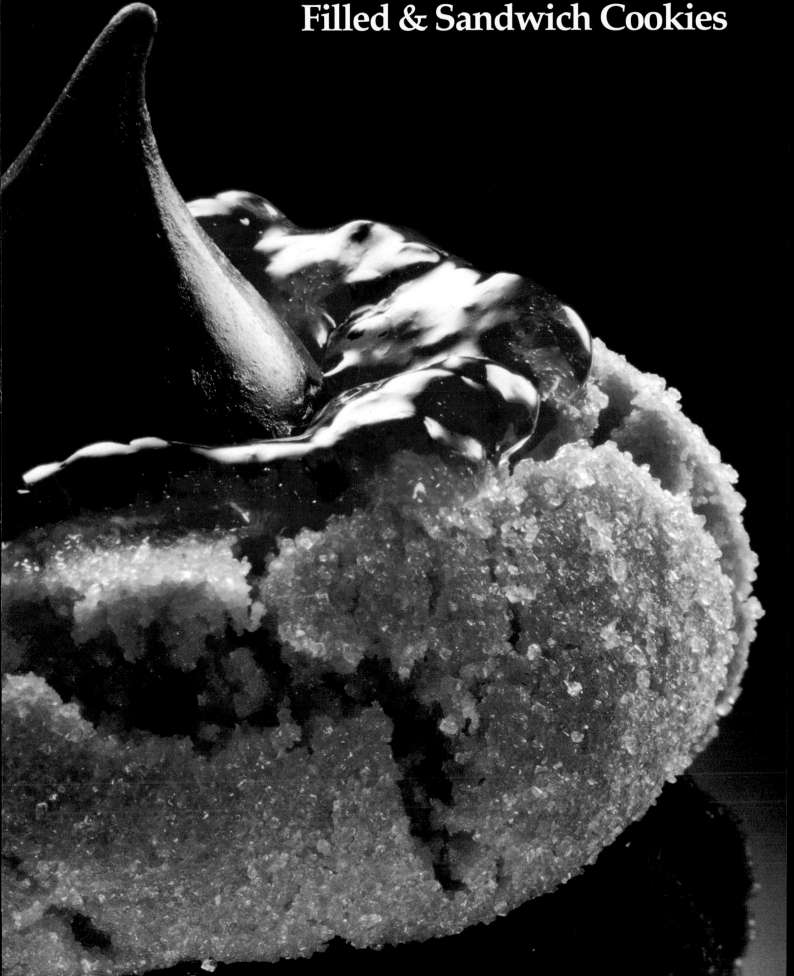

Filled & Sandwich Cookie Basics

These specialty cookies come in a variety of shapes, sizes and flavors. Filled and sandwich cookies can be rolled, hand shaped or dropped, then topped, filled or spread with a flavorful frosting, jam or fruit mixture. These cookies can even be as simple as purchased cookies teamed with an easy filling.

Store filled and sandwich cookies in single layers between sheets of wax paper in a tightly covered container. Freeze the cookies in single layers after fillings are firm, then wrap them tightly for freezer storage. Or freeze cookies in advance; thaw and fill when ready to serve.

How to Make Thumbprint Cookies

1) Use thumb or the end of a spoon to make indentations in balls of cookie dough.

2) Indent tops of cookies again, immediately after removing them from oven, by gently pressing with the end of a spoon.

Use only the amount of filling required when making sandwich cookies. A small frosting knife or spatula works well. Gently press cookies together to form sandwiches. Let filling set before storing.

Tips for Filled Cookies

Pipe fillings into purchased or homemade cookies, if desired. The mixture should be very smooth, without large pieces of fruit or nuts. Ingredients like thick jams or frostings with coconut may clog the decorating tip of a pastry bag.

Banana Chocolate Cream Sandwiches

1 cup (250 mL) granulated
    sugar
1 cup (250 mL) butter or
    margarine, softened
1/2 cup (125 mL) sliced banana
1 teaspoon (5 mL) vanilla
2 1/3 cups (575 mL) all-purpose
    flour
1/2 cup (125 mL) chopped salted
    peanuts
    Granulated sugar

Filling:

4 cups (1 L) powdered sugar
1/3 cup (75 mL) butter or
    margarine, softened
5 to 6 tablespoons (75 to 90 mL)
    milk
3 tablespoons (50 mL)
    unsweetened cocoa
1 teaspoon (5 mL) vanilla
1/4 teaspoon (1 mL) salt

About 2 dozen cookies

Heat oven to 350°F (180°C). In large mixing bowl, combine 1 cup (250 mL) granulated sugar, 1 cup (250 mL) butter, the banana and 1 teaspoon (5 mL) vanilla. Beat at medium speed of electric mixer until light and fluffy. Add flour. Beat at low speed until soft dough forms. Stir in peanuts.

Shape dough into 1-inch (2.5 cm) balls. Place balls 2 inches (5 cm) apart on ungreased cookie sheets. Flatten balls to 2-inch-diameter (5 cm) circles with bottom of drinking glass, dipping glass in granulated sugar to prevent sticking. Bake for 12 to 15 minutes, or until edges are light golden brown. Cool completely. In medium mixing bowl, combine filling ingredients. Beat at low speed of electric mixer until smooth. Spread about 2 teaspoons (10 mL) filling on bottoms of half of cookies. Gently press bottoms of remaining cookies against filling to form sandwiches.

Filled & Sandwich Cookies

Peanut Butter Prints

1/2 cup (125 mL) sugar
1/2 cup (125 mL) butter or
    margarine, softened
1 square (1 oz./30 g)
    unsweetened baking
    chocolate, melted and
    slightly cooled
1 egg yolk
1 tablespoon (15 mL) milk
1/2 teaspoon (2 mL) vanilla
1 1/4 cups (300 mL) all-purpose
    flour
1/4 teaspoon (1 mL) salt
1/3 cup (75 mL) miniature
    candy-coated semisweet
    chocolate chips
1/3 cup (75 mL) creamy peanut
    butter

Drizzle:

1/3 cup (75 mL) semisweet
    chocolate chips
1/2 teaspoon (2 mL) vegetable
    shortening

2 1/2 dozen cookies

Heat oven to 350°F (180°C). In large mixing bowl, combine sugar, butter, melted chocolate, egg yolk, milk and vanilla. Beat at medium speed of electric mixer until well blended. Add flour and salt. Beat at low speed until soft dough forms. Stir in candy-coated chips.

Shape dough into 1-inch (2.5 cm) balls. Place balls 2 inches (5 cm) apart on ungreased cookie sheets. Indent top of each cookie with thumb. Bake for 8 to 12 minutes, or until set. Immediately indent cookies again. Cool completely. Spoon about 1/2 teaspoon (2 mL) peanut butter into each thumbprint.

In 1-quart (1 L) saucepan, combine drizzle ingredients. Melt over medium heat, stirring constantly. Drizzle mixture over peanut butter. Let dry completely before storing.

Tip: Use end of spoon to make indentation in hot cookies.

Microwave tip: In small mixing bowl, melt drizzle ingredients at 50% (Medium) for 2 1/2 to 5 minutes, stirring after every minute. Continue as directed.

Filled & Sandwich Cookies

Turtles

1 cup (250 mL) butter or
    margarine, softened
3/4 cup (175 mL) packed brown
    sugar
1 egg yolk
2 cups (500 mL) all-purpose
    flour
13 caramels, cut in half
1/2 cup (125 mL) pecan halves,
    chopped into large pieces
2 tablespoons (25 mL)
    miniature semisweet
    chocolate chips

About 2 dozen cookies

In large mixing bowl, combine
butter, sugar and egg yolk.
Beat at medium speed of electric mixer until light and fluffy.
Add flour. Beat at low speed
until soft dough forms. Cover
with plastic wrap. Chill 1 to 2
hours, or until firm.

Heat oven to 350°F (180°C).
Shape 1 rounded measuring
tablespoon (15 mL) dough
around 1 caramel half to form
1½-inch (4 cm) ball. Repeat
with remaining dough and
caramel halves.

Place balls 2 inches (5 cm) apart
on ungreased cookie sheets.
Press pecan pieces into balls to
make legs, heads and tails. Press
chips bottom-sides-up into top
of balls for spots. Bake for 13
to 15 minutes, or until set. Cool
completely on cookie sheets
before storing.

Filled & Sandwich Cookies

Peanut Butter 'n Jelly Blossoms

- 1/2 cup (125 mL) granulated sugar
- 1/2 cup (125 mL) packed brown sugar
- 1/2 cup (125 mL) vegetable shortening
- 1/2 cup (125 mL) creamy peanut butter
- 1 egg
- 1 teaspoon (5 mL) vanilla
- 1 3/4 cups (425 mL) all-purpose flour
- 1/2 teaspoon (2 mL) baking soda
- 1/4 teaspoon (1 mL) salt
  Granulated sugar
- 48 chocolate kisses

Glaze:

- 1/4 cup (50 mL) strawberry jelly
- 1/4 teaspoon (1 mL) vanilla

4 dozen cookies

Heat oven to 375°F (190°C). In large mixing bowl, combine 1/2 cup (125 mL) granulated sugar, the brown sugar, shortening, peanut butter, egg and 1 teaspoon (5 mL) vanilla. Beat at medium speed of electric mixer until light and fluffy. Add flour, baking soda and salt. Beat at low speed until soft dough forms.

Shape dough into 1-inch (2.5 cm) balls. Roll balls in granulated sugar. Place balls 2 inches (5 cm) apart on ungreased cookie sheets. Bake for 10 to 12 minutes, or until light golden brown. Immediately press kiss into center of each cookie. Remove cookies from cookie sheets.

In small bowl, combine glaze ingredients. Spoon 1/2 teaspoon (2 mL) glaze around each kiss. Cool completely before storing.

Filled & Sandwich Cookies

Orange Bites

Filling:

- 2/3 cup (150 mL) granulated sugar
- 1 egg
- 1 teaspoon (5 mL) grated orange peel
- 2 tablespoons (25 mL) fresh orange juice
- 1 tablespoon (15 mL) butter or margarine, softened
- 2 teaspoons (10 mL) cornstarch

- 1 cup (250 mL) butter or margarine, softened
- 1/2 cup (125 mL) powdered sugar
- 2 cups (500 mL) all-purpose flour
- 1 teaspoon (5 mL) grated orange peel
- 1/4 teaspoon (1 mL) salt
  Granulated sugar

About 2 dozen cookies

In 1-quart (1 L) saucepan, combine filling ingredients. Cook over medium heat for 5 to 7 minutes, or until thickened and translucent, stirring constantly. Remove from heat. Cool completely. Set aside.

In large mixing bowl, combine 1 cup (250 mL) butter and the powdered sugar. Beat at medium speed of electric mixer until light and fluffy. Add flour, 1 teaspoon (5 mL) peel and the salt. Beat at low speed until soft dough forms. Cover with plastic wrap. Chill 1 to 2 hours, or until firm.

Heat oven to 400°F (200°C). Shape dough into 1-inch (2.5 cm) balls. Place balls 2 inches (5 cm) apart on ungreased cookie sheets. Flatten balls with bottom of drinking glass, dipping glass in granulated sugar to prevent sticking. Using fork, prick top of each cookie. Bake for 9 to 12 minutes, or until edges are light golden brown. Cool completely.

Spread about 1/2 teaspoon (2 mL) filling on bottoms of half of cookies. Gently press bottoms of remaining cookies against filling to form sandwiches. Store in refrigerator.

Mini Apricot Rolls

Filling:

  1 pkg. (6 oz./170 g) dried
     apricots, finely chopped
 1/2 cup (125 mL) honey
 1/4 cup (50 mL) water
  2 tablespoons (25 mL) lemon
     juice

 1/2 cup (125 mL) sugar
 1/2 cup (125 mL) butter or
     margarine, softened
 1/2 cup (125 mL) honey
  1 egg
  1 teaspoon (5 mL) vanilla
23/4 cups (675 mL) all-purpose
     flour
 3/4 cup (175 mL) whole wheat
     flour
 1/2 teaspoon (2 mL) baking soda
 1/4 teaspoon (1 mL) salt

     81/2 dozen cookies

In 1-quart (1 L) saucepan, combine filling ingredients. Cook over medium-high heat for 8 to 11 minutes, or until thickened, stirring constantly. Cool completely. Set aside.

Heat oven to 350°F (180°C). In large mixing bowl, combine sugar, butter, 1/2 cup (125 mL) honey, the egg and vanilla. Beat at medium speed of electric mixer until light and fluffy. Add flours, baking soda and salt. Beat at low speed until soft dough forms.

Divide dough in half. On floured wax paper, roll half of dough into 12 x 9-inch (30 x 23 cm) rectangle. Using sharp knife or pastry wheel, cut dough into 3 x 1-inch (8 x 2.5 cm) strips. Place rounded 1/2 teaspoon (2 mL) filling onto center of each strip. Overlap ends of strips over filling to form 1-inch (2.5 cm) square rolls.

Place rolls seam-sides-down 1 inch (2.5 cm) apart on ungreased cookie sheets. Repeat with remaining dough and filling. Bake for 11 to 14 minutes, or until edges are light golden brown. Cool completely before storing.

Variation: Mini Fig Rolls: Substitute 11/4 cups (300 mL) whole dried figs for dried apricots and 2 tablespoons (25 mL) orange juice for lemon juice. In food processor or blender, process figs until smooth. In 1-quart (1 L) saucepan, combine figs and remaining filling ingredients. Cook over medium-high heat for 5 to 7 minutes, or until thickened, stirring constantly. Continue as directed.

Filled & Sandwich Cookies

Cranberry Lemon Sandwiches (top center)

1 cup (250 mL) granulated sugar
1 cup (250 mL) powdered sugar
1 cup (250 mL) butter or margarine, softened
1 cup (250 mL) vegetable shortening
2 eggs
2 teaspoons (10 mL) vanilla
4 cups (1 L) all-purpose flour
1 teaspoon (5 mL) cream of tartar
1 teaspoon (5 mL) grated lemon peel
1/2 teaspoon (2 mL) salt
3/4 cup (175 mL) chopped dried cranberries
    Granulated sugar

Filling:

2 3/4 cups (675 mL) powdered sugar
2/3 cup (150 mL) butter or margarine, softened
4 to 6 tablespoons (50 to 90 mL) whipping cream
1 1/4 teaspoons (6 mL) grated lemon peel

About 6 dozen cookies

In large mixing bowl, combine 1 cup (250 mL) granulated sugar, 1 cup (250 mL) powdered sugar, 1 cup (250 mL) butter, the shortening, eggs and vanilla. Beat at high speed of electric mixer until light and fluffy. Add flour, cream of tartar, 1 teaspoon (5 mL) peel and the salt. Beat at low speed until soft dough forms. Stir in cranberries. Cover with plastic wrap. Chill 1 to 2 hours, or until firm.

Heat oven to 350°F (180°C). Shape dough into 1/2-inch (1 cm) balls. Place balls 2 inches (5 cm) apart on ungreased cookie sheets. Flatten balls with bottom of drinking glass, dipping glass in granulated sugar to prevent sticking. Bake for 10 to 13 minutes, or until edges are light golden brown. Cool completely.

In small bowl, combine filling ingredients. Beat at low speed of electric mixer until smooth. Spread about 2 teaspoons (10 mL) filling on bottoms of half of cookies. Gently press bottoms of remaining cookies against filling to form sandwiches.

Cherry Blossoms (top left)

2 cups (500 mL) all-purpose flour
1 cup (250 mL) butter or margarine, softened
1/3 cup (75 mL) whipping cream
1 1/2 teaspoons (7 mL) cherry extract
1/2 teaspoon (2 mL) red food coloring
    Granulated sugar

Filling:

2 cups (500 mL) powdered sugar
1/2 cup (125 mL) butter or margarine, softened
2 tablespoons (25 mL) milk
1/2 teaspoon (2 mL) cherry extract

4 1/2 dozen cookies

In large mixing bowl, combine flour, 1 cup (250 mL) butter, the cream, 1 1/2 teaspoons (7 mL) cherry extract and the food coloring. Beat at low speed of electric mixer until soft dough forms. Divide dough into thirds. Cover with plastic wrap. Chill 1 to 2 hours, or until firm.

Heat oven to 375°F (190°C). On well-floured surface, roll one third of dough to 1/8-inch (3 mm) thickness. Using 2 1/2-inch (6 cm) flower cookie cutter, cut shapes into dough. Dip both sides of shapes in granulated sugar. Place shapes 2 inches (5 cm) apart on ungreased cookie sheets. Repeat with remaining dough. Using fork, prick top of each shape. Bake for 5 to 8 minutes, or until puffy but not brown. Cool completely.

In small mixing bowl, combine filling ingredients. Beat at low speed of electric mixer until smooth. Spread about 1/2 teaspoon (2 mL) filling on bottoms of half of cookies. Gently press bottoms of remaining cookies against filling to form sandwiches.

Almond Tart Cookies

1⅓ cups (325 mL) all-purpose
    flour
½ cup (125 mL) granulated
    sugar
⅓ cup (75 mL) butter or
    margarine, softened
1 egg
½ teaspoon (2 mL) vanilla

Filling:
¾ cup (175 mL) packed brown
    sugar
½ cup (125 mL) chopped
    almonds
⅓ cup (75 mL) miniature
    semisweet chocolate chips
1 egg, slightly beaten
1 tablespoon (15 mL) butter or
    margarine, melted
½ teaspoon (2 mL) almond
    extract or 1 teaspoon (5 mL)
    almond-flavored liqueur

2 dozen cookies

Heat oven to 350°F (180°C). In
large mixing bowl, combine
flour, granulated sugar, ⅓ cup
(75 mL) butter, 1 egg and the
vanilla. Beat at low speed of
electric mixer until mixture
resembles coarse crumbs. Into
each cup of 2 ungreased 12-cup
miniature muffin pans, press
1 tablespoon (15 mL) crumb
mixture to form shells.

In medium mixing bowl, combine filling ingredients. Fill
each shell ¾ full with filling.
(Do not overfill.) Bake for 25
to 27 minutes, or until set. Let
cool for 10 minutes before
removing from pans. Cool
completely before storing.

Creamy Peach-filled Walnut Cookies

1   cup (250 mL) granulated
    sugar
3/4 cup (175 mL) butter or
    margarine, softened
1   teaspoon (5 mL) vanilla
1 1/2 cups (375 mL) all-purpose
    flour
1/4 teaspoon (1 mL) salt
3/4 cup (175 mL) chopped
    walnuts
    Granulated sugar

Filling:

1 1/2 cups (375 mL) powdered
    sugar
1   pkg. (3 oz./85 g) cream
    cheese, softened
1/3 cup (75 mL) peach preserves
1   teaspoon (5 mL)
    peach-flavored liqueur

                1 1/2 dozen cookies

Heat oven to 350°F (180°C). In large mixing bowl, combine 1 cup (250 mL) granulated sugar, the butter and vanilla. Beat at medium speed of electric mixer until light and fluffy. Add flour and salt. Beat at low speed until soft dough forms. Stir in walnuts.

Shape dough into 1-inch (2.5 cm) balls. Roll balls in granulated sugar. Place balls 2 inches (5 cm) apart on ungreased cookie sheets. Flatten balls with fork in crisscross pattern. Bake for 12 to 15 minutes, or until edges are light golden brown. Cool completely.

In medium mixing bowl, combine filling ingredients. Beat at low speed of electric mixer until smooth. Spread about 2 teaspoons (10 mL) filling on bottoms of half of cookies. Gently press bottoms of remaining cookies against filling to form sandwiches.

Prune-filled Cookies

       1 cup (250 mL) granulated sugar
     1/2 cup (125 mL) vegetable shortening
       2 eggs
     1/3 cup (75 mL) milk
       1 teaspoon (5 mL) vanilla
    3 1/4 cups (800 mL) all-purpose flour
       1 teaspoon (5 mL) baking soda
     1/4 teaspoon (1 mL) salt

Filling:

    1 1/3 cups (325 mL) chopped pitted prunes
     1/3 cup (75 mL) apricot preserves

Drizzle:

       1 cup (250 mL) powdered sugar
       1 to 2 tablespoons (15 to 25 mL) milk
     1/4 teaspoon (1 mL) vanilla

8 1/2 dozen cookies

Heat oven to 375°F (190°C). In large mixing bowl, combine granulated sugar, shortening, eggs, 1/3 cup (75 mL) milk and 1 teaspoon (5 mL) vanilla. Beat at medium speed of electric mixer until well blended. Add flour, baking soda and salt. Beat at low speed until soft dough forms.

On floured surface, roll dough to 1/4-inch (5 mm) thickness. Using 2-inch (5 cm) round cookie cutter, cut circles into dough. Place half of circles 2 inches (5 cm) apart on ungreased cookie sheets.

Combine filling ingredients in small mixing bowl. Spoon about 1/2 teaspoon (2 mL) filling onto center of each circle on cookie sheets. Place remaining circles over filling. Press edges with fork dipped in flour to seal. Bake for 10 to 13 minutes, or until edges are light golden brown. Cool completely.

In small mixing bowl, combine drizzle ingredients. Pipe or drizzle mixture over cookies. Let dry completely before storing.

Filled & Sandwich Cookies

Buttery Plum-filled Turnovers

2/3 cup (150 mL) butter or
    margarine, softened
1/2 cup (125 mL) granulated
    sugar
1 egg
2 tablespoons (25 mL) milk
1 teaspoon (5 mL) vanilla
2 1/2 cups (625 mL) all-purpose
    flour
1/4 teaspoon (1 mL) baking soda
1/4 teaspoon (1 mL) salt
3/4 cup (175 mL) plum preserves
1/2 cup (125 mL) chopped pecans
    Powdered sugar

About 2 dozen cookies

Heat oven to 350°F (180°C). In large mixing bowl, combine butter, granulated sugar, egg, milk and vanilla. Beat at medium speed of electric mixer until light and fluffy. Add flour, baking soda and salt. Beat at low speed until soft dough forms.

On floured surface, roll dough to 1/4-inch (5 mm) thickness. Using 3-inch (8 cm) square cookie cutter, cut shapes into dough. Place shapes 2 inches (5 cm) apart on ungreased cookie sheets.

In small mixing bowl, combine preserves and pecans. Spoon 1/2 teaspoon (2 mL) preserves mixture onto center of each square.

Fold squares over mixture to form triangles. Press edges with fork dipped in flour to seal. Using knife, pierce tops of triangles. Bake for 11 to 14 minutes, or until edges are light golden brown. Sprinkle with powdered sugar. Cool completely before storing.

Filled & Sandwich Cookies

Chocolate Caramel Balls

 1 pkg. (8 oz./227 g) cream cheese, softened,
   divided
¹/2 cup (125 mL) packed brown sugar
¹/2 cup (125 mL) butter or margarine, softened
¹/4 cup (50 mL) granulated sugar
 1 egg
 1 teaspoon (5 mL) vanilla
 2 cups (500 mL) all-purpose flour
¹/4 cup (50 mL) unsweetened cocoa
 1 teaspoon (5 mL) baking powder
18 caramels, cut in half

Frosting:
1¹/2 cups (375 mL) powdered sugar
  2 tablespoons (25 mL) unsweetened cocoa
  2 tablespoons (25 mL) caramel ice cream topping
  2 to 3 teaspoons (10 to 15 mL) milk

3 dozen cookies

Heat oven to 350°F (180°C). In large mixing bowl, combine 6 oz. (175 g) cream cheese, the brown sugar, butter, granulated sugar, egg and vanilla. Beat at medium speed of electric mixer until light and fluffy. Add flour, ¹/4 cup (50 mL) cocoa and the baking powder. Beat at low speed until soft dough forms.

Shape 1 measuring tablespoon (15 mL) dough around 1 caramel half to form 1-inch (2.5 cm) ball. Repeat with remaining dough and caramel halves. Place balls 2 inches (5 cm) apart on un-greased cookie sheets. Bake for 10 to 14 minutes, or until set. Cool completely.

In small mixing bowl, combine remaining cream cheese and the frosting ingredients. Beat at low speed of electric mixer until smooth. Spread frosting evenly on cookies. Let dry completely before storing.

Hazelnut Sandwich Cookies

    1 cup (250 mL) granulated sugar
  3/4 cup (175 mL) butter or margarine, softened
    1 pkg. (3 oz./85 g) cream cheese, softened
  1/4 cup (50 mL) sour cream
    1 egg
    1 tablespoon (15 mL) hazelnut liqueur
2 3/4 cups (675 mL) all-purpose flour
    1 teaspoon (5 mL) baking powder
  1/3 cup (75 mL) finely chopped hazelnuts
    Granulated sugar

Filling:
1 1/2 cups (375 mL) powdered sugar
  3/4 cup (175 mL) milk chocolate chips, melted and
      slightly cooled
    3 to 5 tablespoons (50 to 75 mL) milk

About 2 1/2 dozen cookies

In large mixing bowl, combine 1 cup (250 mL) granulated sugar, the butter, cream cheese, sour cream, egg and liqueur. Beat at medium speed of electric mixer until well blended. Add flour and baking powder. Beat at low speed until soft dough forms. Stir in hazelnuts. Cover with plastic wrap. Chill 2 to 3 hours, or until firm.

Heat oven to 350°F (180°C). Shape dough into 1-inch (2.5 cm) balls. Roll balls in granulated sugar. Place balls 2 inches (5 cm) apart on ungreased cookie sheets. Flatten balls with bottom of drinking glass, dipping glass in additional granulated sugar to prevent sticking. Bake for 8 to 11 minutes, or until set. Cool completely.

In small mixing bowl, combine filling ingredients. Beat at high speed of electric mixer until light and fluffy. Spread about 2 teaspoons (10 mL) filling on bottoms of half of cookies. Gently press bottoms of remaining cookies against filling to form sandwiches.

Fruit-filled Freezer Cookies

4 oz. (125 g) white or
   chocolate-flavored candy
   coating
½ teaspoon (2 mL) vegetable
   shortening
24 assorted cookies (1½ to
   2-inch/4 to 5 cm)
   Fresh strawberry slices
   Fresh raspberries
   Mandarin orange segments

1 dozen cookies

Line cookie sheet with wax paper. Set aside. In 1-quart (1 L) saucepan, combine candy coating and shortening. Melt over low heat, stirring constantly. Spoon small amount of coating onto bottoms of half of cookies.

Place cookies coated-sides-up on prepared cookie sheet. Arrange 2 or 3 strawberry slices, 4 raspberries or 2 orange segments in coating on cookies. Spoon small amount of coating over fruit.

Gently press bottoms of remaining cookies against filling to form sandwiches. Drizzle remaining coating over cookies. Freeze until set. Place cookies in large plastic food-storage bag and store in freezer.

Microwave tip: In small mixing bowl, melt candy coating and shortening at 50% (Medium) for 2 to 4 minutes, stirring after every minute. Continue as directed.

Filled & Sandwich Cookies

Fancy Filled Cookies

1 cup (250 mL) ready-to-spread
   frosting
1 pkg. (5½ oz./156 g)
   pirouette cookies
4 oz. (125 g) white or
   chocolate-flavored candy
   coating
½ teaspoon (2 mL) vegetable
   shortening
   Red or green colored sugar
   (optional)
   Multicolored shot (optional)

2 dozen cookies

Line cookie sheets with wax
paper. Set aside. Place frosting
in 1-quart (1 L) sealable freezer
bag. Squeeze frosting to corner
of bag. Seal bag. Using scissors, snip corner slightly to
form tip. Pipe frosting into
both ends of each cookie.
Place cookies on prepared
cookie sheets. Set aside.

In 1-quart (1 L) saucepan, combine candy coating and shortening. Melt over low heat,
stirring constantly. Spoon coating into second 1-quart (1 L)
sealable freezer bag. Squeeze
coating to corner of bag. Seal
bag. Using scissors, snip corner
slightly to form writing tip.

Pipe coating over cookies in
zigzig or other decorative pattern. (Note: A pastry bag with
a fine tip may also be used for
piping frosting and coating.)
Sprinkle with sugar or shot. Let
dry completely before storing.

Microwave tip: In small mixing bowl, melt candy coating
and shortening at 50% (Medium) for 2 to 4 minutes, stirring
after every minute. Continue
as directed.

Filled & Sandwich Cookies

Holiday & Special-occasion Cookies

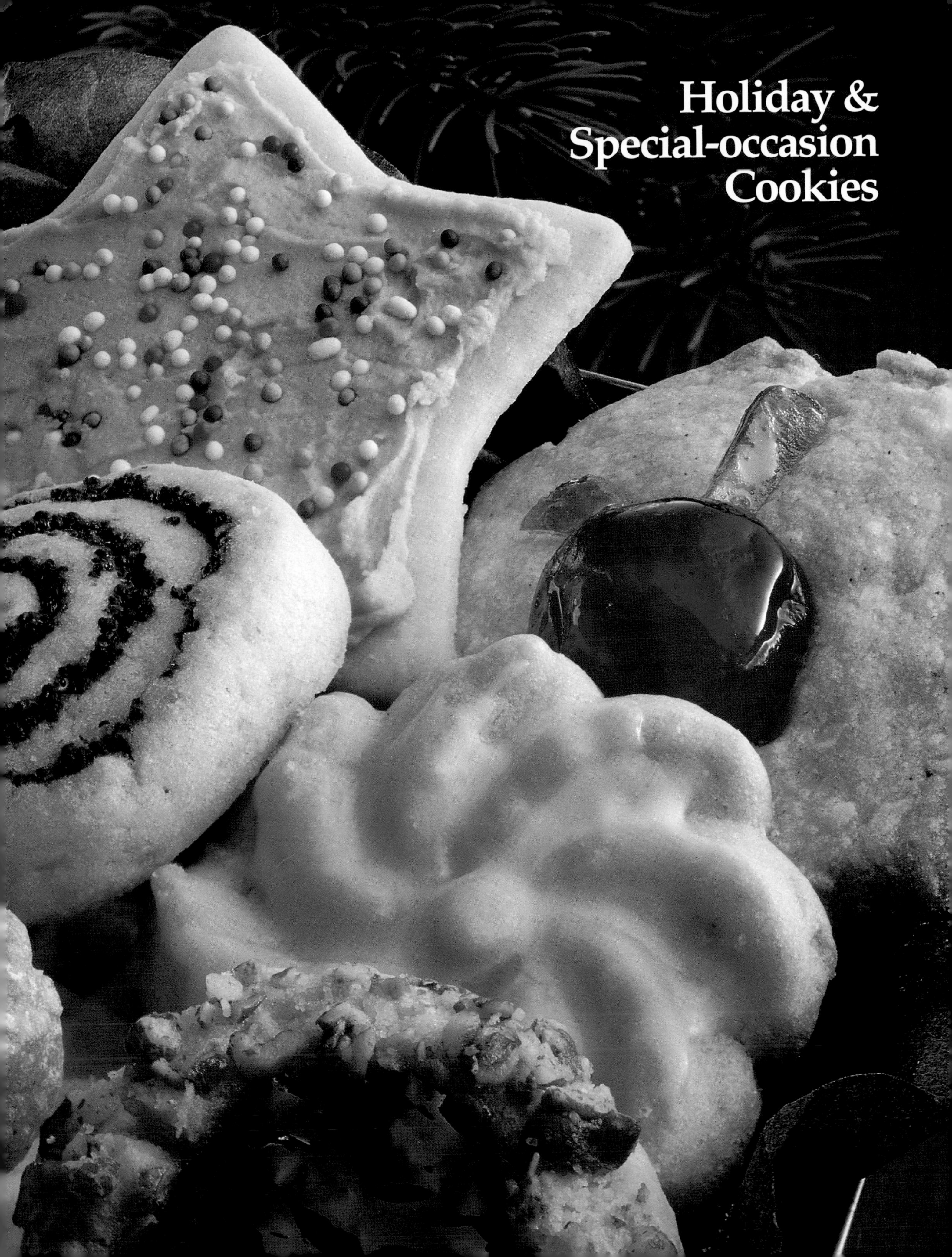

Holiday & Special-occasion Cookie Basics

This collection of holiday and special-occasion cookies has recipes from a variety of countries. Austrian bakers get the credit for creating rich, buttery Florentines. These chocolate-glazed specialties are traditionally a mixture of honey, butter, sugar and candied fruit. Pfeffernüsse, or "peppernuts," are spicy cookies that are served at Christmastime in Germany. And Fattigmands are a crispy fried Scandinavian specialty, also a Christmas favorite. Italian Biscotti can be served any time. These intensely flavored cookies are twice-baked, making them crunchy and perfect for dipping in coffee or a sweet dessert wine.

Some of these recipes require specialized equipment, which is available at specialty cooking or kitchen stores.

Madeleine pans: These pans have special scallop-shell indentations for the cookies' signature look.

Cookie cutters: In a few recipes, we call for special cookie cutters. These can be found in many stores, or you can make your own (see page 32).

Madeleine pan

Rosette iron

Special cookie cutters

Rosette irons: A heatproof handle is attached to one or two long metal rods. Various decorative forms can be attached to the rods. The forms are dipped in batter, then lowered into hot oil.

Krumkake and pizzelle irons: Krumkake and pizzelles are baked on the stovetop in hinged irons that leave designs on the thinly pressed cookies. Freshly made krumkake are shaped around a special **cone.** Pizzelles are served flat.

Krumkake iron

Krumkake cone

Pizzelle iron

Special-occasion Sugar Cookies

 1 cup (250 mL) sugar, *divided*
³/4 cup (175 mL) butter or margarine, *softened*
 1 egg
 3 tablespoons (50 mL) whipping cream
 1 teaspoon (5 mL) vanilla
 1 teaspoon (5 mL) almond extract
 3 cups (750 mL) all-purpose flour
1¹/2 teaspoons (7 mL) baking powder
 ¹/2 teaspoon (2 mL) salt
   Granulated sugar
   Decorator Frosting (see page 246)

5¹/2 dozen cookies

In large mixing bowl, combine 1 cup (250 mL) sugar, the butter, egg, whipping cream, vanilla and almond extract. Beat at medium speed of electric mixer until light and fluffy. Add flour, baking powder and salt. Beat at low speed until soft dough forms. Cover with plastic wrap. Chill 1 to 2 hours, or until firm.

Heat oven to 400°F (200°C). On floured surface, roll dough to ¹/4-inch (5 mm) thickness. Using 3-inch (8 cm) cookie cutters, cut desired shapes into dough. Place shapes 2 inches (5 cm) apart on ungreased cookie sheets. Sprinkle shapes with sugar. Bake for 4 to 6 minutes, or until edges are light golden brown. Prepare frosting as directed. Decorate cookies as desired. Let dry completely before storing.

Sour Cream Cutouts

2   *cups (500 mL) sugar*
1   *cup (250 mL) sour cream*
3   *eggs*
1/2 *cup (125 mL) butter or margarine, softened*
1/2 *cup (125 mL) vegetable shortening*
5 1/2 *cups (1.375 L) all-purpose flour*
2   *teaspoons (10 mL) baking powder*
2   *teaspoons (10 mL) baking soda*
1   *teaspoon (5 mL) vanilla*
1   *teaspoon (5 mL) almond extract*
1/4 *teaspoon (1 mL) salt*
    Decorator Frosting (see page 246)

About 10 dozen cookies

In large mixing bowl, combine sugar, sour cream, eggs, butter and shortening. Beat at medium speed of electric mixer until light and fluffy. Add flour, baking powder, baking soda, vanilla, almond extract and salt. Beat at low speed until soft dough forms. Cover with plastic wrap. Chill 1 to 2 hours, or until firm.

Heat oven to 350°F (180°C). On well-floured surface, roll dough to 1/4-inch (5 mm) thickness. Using 3-inch (8 cm) cookie cutters, cut desired shapes into dough. Place shapes 2 inches (5 cm) apart on ungreased cookie sheets. Bake for 6 to 8 minutes, or until edges are light golden brown. Prepare frosting as directed. Decorate cookies as desired. Let dry completely before storing.

Holiday & Special-occasion Cookies

Russian Tea Cakes

1 cup (250 mL) butter or
  margarine, softened
1/2 cup (125 mL) powdered
  sugar
1/2 teaspoon (2 mL) vanilla
1/2 teaspoon (2 mL) almond
  extract
21/4 cups (550 mL) all-purpose
  flour
1/4 teaspoon (1 mL) salt
3/4 cup (175 mL) finely chopped
  pecans
  Powdered sugar

31/2 dozen cookies

Heat oven to 400°F (200°C). In
large mixing bowl, combine
butter, 1/2 cup (125 mL) sugar,
the vanilla and almond extract.
Beat at medium speed of electric mixer until light and fluffy.
Add flour and salt. Beat at low
speed until soft dough forms.
Stir in pecans.

Shape dough into 1-inch (2.5 cm)
balls. Place balls 2 inches (5 cm)
apart on ungreased cookie
sheets. Bake for 10 to 12 minutes, or until set. Immediately
roll cookies in powdered
sugar. Cool completely. Reroll
cookies in powdered sugar
before storing.

Cookie Nests

3 cups (750 mL) chow mein noodles
1 cup (250 mL) miniature candy-coated
    semisweet chocolate pieces
1 jar (7 oz./196 g) marshmallow cream
¼ cup (50 mL) chunky peanut butter
¼ cup (50 mL) flaked coconut
2 tablespoons (25 mL) butter or margarine, softened
1 teaspoon (5 mL) vanilla
    Small gumdrops or jelly beans (optional)

In large mixing bowl, combine all ingredients, except gumdrops. Cover with plastic wrap. Chill 15 to 20 minutes for easier handling.

With greased hands, form ¼ cup (50 mL) mixture into nest shape. Repeat with remaining mixture. Place nests on wax paper. Let dry. Fill nests with gumdrops before serving.

15 nests

Holiday & Special-occasion Cookies

Poppy Seed Pinwheels (top)

1/2 cup (125 mL) butter or margarine, softened
1/4 cup (50 mL) granulated sugar
1 egg
1 teaspoon (5 mL) grated orange peel
1 teaspoon (5 mL) vanilla
1 1/2 cups (375 mL) all-purpose flour
1/2 teaspoon (2 mL) baking soda
1 cup (250 mL) poppy seed filling, divided
  Powdered sugar (optional)

4 dozen cookies

In large mixing bowl, combine butter, granulated sugar, egg, peel and vanilla. Beat at medium speed of electric mixer until light and fluffy. Add flour and baking soda. Beat at low speed until soft dough forms. Divide dough in half. Cover with plastic wrap. Chill 30 minutes to 1 hour, or until firm.

Roll half of dough between 2 sheets of wax paper into 12 x 10-inch (30 x 25 cm) rectangle. Repeat with remaining dough. Chill 30 minutes.

Heat oven to 350°F (180°C). Lightly grease cookie sheets. Set aside. Discard top sheet of wax paper from first half dough. Spread 1/2 cup (125 mL) filling to within 1/4 inch (5 mm) of edges. Roll dough jelly roll style, starting with long side. (Peel off wax paper when rolling.) Pinch edge to seal. Repeat with remaining dough and 1/2 cup (125 mL) filling.

Cut rolls into 1/2-inch (1 cm) slices. Place slices 2 inches (5 cm) apart on prepared cookie sheets. Bake for 10 to 12 minutes, or until edges are light golden brown. Cool completely. Sprinkle pinwheels with powdered sugar.

Optional Glaze:

1 cup (250 mL) powdered sugar
1 to 2 tablespoons (15 to 25 mL) orange juice

In small mixing bowl, combine sugar and juice. Stir until smooth. Drizzle over cooled pinwheels.

Holiday Thumbprint Cookies (bottom)

1 cup (250 mL) butter or margarine, softened
1/2 cup (125 mL) packed brown sugar
2 eggs, separated
2 cups (500 mL) all-purpose flour
1 teaspoon (5 mL) water
1 1/2 cups (375 mL) finely chopped pecans
3 tablespoons (50 mL) currant jelly or other tart jelly

3 dozen cookies

Heat oven to 300°F (150°C). In large mixing bowl, combine butter, sugar and egg yolks. Beat at medium speed of electric mixer until light and fluffy. Add flour. Beat at low speed until soft dough forms. Set aside.

In small mixing bowl, beat egg whites and water at high speed until foamy. Set aside.

Shape dough into 1-inch (2.5 cm) balls. Dip balls into egg white mixture. Roll balls in pecans. Place balls 2 inches (5 cm) apart on ungreased cookie sheets. Indent top of each cookie with thumb. Bake for 18 to 20 minutes, or until set.

Immediately indent cookies again. Spoon 1/4 teaspoon (1 mL) jelly into each thumbprint. Cool completely before storing. (Do not stack cookies.)

Tip: Use end of spoon to make indentation in hot cookies.

Cocoa Peppermint Pretzels

1 cup (250 mL) powdered sugar
1 cup (250 mL) butter or margarine, softened
1 egg
1½ teaspoons (7 mL) vanilla
2½ cups (625 mL) all-purpose flour
½ cup (125 mL) unsweetened cocoa
½ teaspoon (2 mL) salt
½ cup (125 mL) vanilla baking chips
1 teaspoon (5 mL) vegetable shortening
12 hard peppermint candies, crushed

4 dozen cookies

In large mixing bowl, combine sugar, butter, egg and vanilla. Beat at medium speed of electric mixer until light and fluffy. Add flour, cocoa and salt. Beat at low speed until soft dough forms. Cover with plastic wrap. Chill 2 to 3 hours, or until firm.

Heat oven to 375°F (190°C). Shape level measuring tablespoons (15 mL) dough into 9-inch-long (23 cm) ropes. Twist ropes into pretzel shapes. Place pretzels 2 inches (5 cm) apart on ungreased cookie sheets. Bake for 8 to 9 minutes, or until set. Cool completely.

Line cookie sheets with wax paper. Set aside. In 1-quart (1 L) saucepan, combine chips and shortening. Melt over low heat, stirring constantly. Dip one end of each pretzel into melted chips, then roll dipped ends into crushed candies. Place pretzels on prepared cookie sheets. Let dry completely before storing.

Microwave tip: In small mixing bowl, melt chips and shortening at 50% (Medium) for 2 to 4 minutes, stirring after every minute. Continue as directed.

Mint Truffle Cookies

1¼ cups (300 mL) sugar
  1 cup (250 mL) butter or margarine, softened
  2 eggs
  1 teaspoon (5 mL) vanilla
2½ cups (625 mL) all-purpose flour
  ¼ cup (50 mL) unsweetened cocoa
  1 teaspoon (5 mL) baking powder
  ¼ teaspoon (1 mL) salt
  1 pkg. (4.67 oz./132 g) chocolate sandwich
    mints, coarsely chopped

Glaze:
  8 oz. (250 g) white candy coating
  1 teaspoon (5 mL) vegetable shortening
  1 or 2 drops green food coloring

4 dozen cookies

In large mixing bowl, combine sugar, butter, eggs and vanilla. Beat at medium speed of electric mixer until light and fluffy. Add flour, cocoa, baking powder and salt. Beat at low speed until soft dough forms. Stir in mints. Cover with plastic wrap. Chill 2 to 3 hours, or until firm.

Heat oven to 375°F (190°C). Lightly grease cookie sheets. Shape dough into 1-inch (2.5 cm) balls. Place balls 2 inches (5 cm) apart on prepared cookie sheets. Bake for 8 to 10 minutes, or until set. Cool completely.

In 1-quart (1 L) saucepan, combine candy coating and shortening. Melt over low heat, stirring constantly. Stir in food coloring. Pipe or drizzle glaze over cookies to form stripes. Let dry completely before storing.

Microwave tip: In small mixing bowl, melt candy coating and shortening at 50% (Medium) for 2 to 4 minutes, stirring after every minute. Continue as directed.

Holiday Special-occasion Cookies

Brandied Ginger Snaps

1/2 cup (125 mL) granulated sugar
1/2 cup (125 mL) butter or margarine
1/3 cup (75 mL) dark molasses
1 tablespoon (15 mL) apricot-flavored brandy
13/4 to 2 cups (425 to 500 mL) all-purpose flour,
    divided
1 teaspoon (5 mL) pumpkin pie spice
    Pinch of salt

Frosting:
2 cups (500 mL) powdered sugar
1/4 cup (50 mL) caramel ice cream topping
1 to 2 teaspoons (5 to 10 mL) milk
1/2 teaspoon (2 mL) vanilla

About 31/2 dozen cookies

Heat oven to 350°F (180°C). Lightly grease cookie sheets. Set aside. In 1-quart (1 L) saucepan, combine granulated sugar, butter and molasses. Bring to boil over medium heat, stirring constantly. Boil for 1 minute. Remove from heat. Stir in brandy. Set aside.

In large mixing bowl, combine 11/4 cups (300 mL) flour, the pumpkin pie spice and salt. Add butter mixture. Beat at medium speed of electric mixer until well blended. Stir or knead in enough of remaining 3/4 cup (175 mL) flour to form stiff dough.

On prepared cookie sheet, roll out two-thirds dough to 1/8 to 1/4-inch (3 to 5 mm) thickness. Using 3-inch (8 cm) leaf-shaped cookie cutter, cut shapes into dough at 1/2-inch (1 cm) intervals. Remove scraps and knead into remaining dough. Repeat with remaining dough on additional prepared cookie sheets. Bake for 7 to 8 minutes, or until set. Cool completely.

In small mixing bowl, combine frosting ingredients. Beat at high speed of electric mixer until smooth. Pipe leaf outline on cookies, or frost cookies with thin layer of frosting. Let dry completely before storing.

Holiday Horns

- ½ cup (125 mL) *butter or margarine, softened*
- 1 pkg. (3 oz./85 g) *cream cheese, softened*
- 1⅓ cups (325 mL) *all-purpose flour*
- 2 tablespoons (25 mL) *sugar*
- 1 tablespoon (15 mL) *milk*
- ½ teaspoon (2 mL) *vanilla*
- ½ cup (125 mL) *favorite red jelly*
- ½ cup (125 mL) *finely chopped pistachios*

4 dozen cookies

In small mixing bowl, combine butter and cream cheese. Beat at medium speed of electric mixer until light and fluffy. Add flour, sugar, milk and vanilla. Beat at low speed until soft dough forms. Cover with plastic wrap. Chill 4 to 5 hours, or until firm.

Heat oven to 325°F (160°C). Lightly grease cookie sheets. Set aside. Divide dough into quarters. On floured surface, roll one quarter dough to ⅛-inch (3 mm) thickness. Using 2-inch (5 cm) round cookie cutter, cut circles into dough. Place circles 2 inches (5 cm) apart on prepared cookie sheets.

Spoon ¼ teaspoon (1 mL) jelly onto center of each circle. Sprinkle ½ teaspoon (2 mL) pistachios over jelly on each circle. Lightly brush edges with water.

Fold opposite edges over filling and pinch together to form cone. Repeat with remaining dough, jelly and pistachios. Bake for 13 to 15 minutes, or until golden brown. Cool completely before storing.

Tip: If dough becomes too sticky to roll, refrigerate until firm.

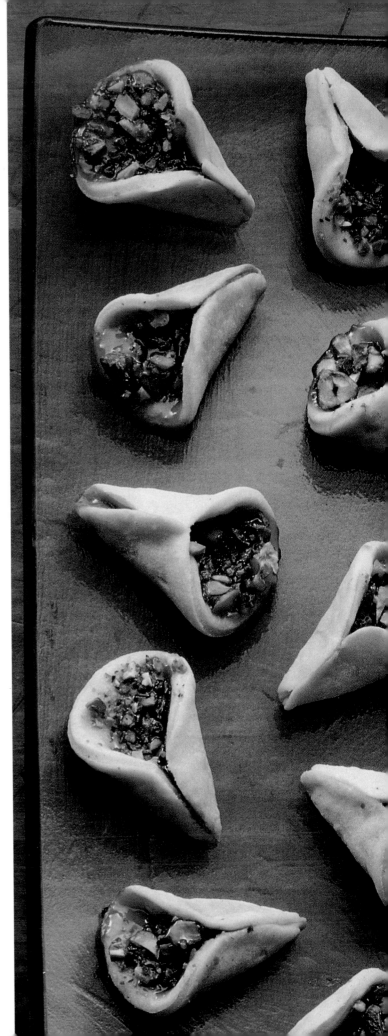

Appliquéd Almond Cookies

3/4 cup (175 mL) butter or
    margarine, softened
1/3 cup (75 mL) almond paste
1 cup (250 mL) granulated
    sugar
1 egg
3 tablespoons (50 mL) milk
1 teaspoon (5 mL) almond
    extract
3 cups (750 mL) all-purpose
    flour
1 1/2 teaspoons (7 mL) baking
    powder
1/2 teaspoon (2 mL) salt
    Food coloring
    Coarse sugar crystals

6 dozen cookies

In large mixing bowl, combine butter and almond paste. Beat at medium speed of electric mixer until smooth. Add granulated sugar, egg, milk and almond extract. Beat at medium speed until well blended. Add flour, baking powder and salt. Beat at low speed until soft dough forms. Divide dough into thirds. Cover 2/3 dough with plastic wrap. Add food coloring, one drop at a time, to remaining 1/3 dough, kneading dough until color is equally distributed and dough is desired shade. Cover with plastic wrap. Chill all dough 2 to 3 hours, or until firm.

Heat oven to 400°F (200°C). On floured surface, roll half of uncolored dough to 1/8-inch (3 mm) thickness. Using 2 1/4-inch (6 cm) round cookie cutter, cut circles into dough. Place circles 2 inches (5 cm) apart on ungreased cookie sheets. Set aside.

On floured surface, roll half of colored dough to 1/8-inch (3 mm) thickness. Using 2-inch (5 cm) cutter of desired shape (see Decorating Tip), cut shapes into dough. Place one colored shape on top of each uncolored circle. Repeat with remaining colored and uncolored dough. Sprinkle shapes with sugar crystals. Bake for 5 to 7 minutes, or until edges are golden brown. Cool completely before storing.

Decorating Tip: Use red hearts for Valentine's Day, yellow stars or bells for Christmas, multicolored bunnies or eggs for Easter, green shamrocks for St. Patrick's Day, etc.

Lemon Blossom Spritz

  1 *cup (250 mL) butter or margarine, softened*
  1/2 *cup (125 mL) granulated sugar*
  1/2 *cup (125 mL) packed brown sugar*
  1 *egg*
  1 *teaspoon (5 mL) grated lemon peel*
  1 *tablespoon (15 mL) fresh lemon juice*
  1 *teaspoon (5 mL) vanilla*
2 1/2 *cups (625 mL) all-purpose flour*
  1/4 *teaspoon (1 mL) baking soda*
  1/4 *teaspoon (1 mL) salt*

Frosting:

1 1/4 *cups (300 mL) powdered sugar*
  1/2 *teaspoon (2 mL) grated lemon peel*
  2 *to 4 teaspoons (10 to 20 mL) fresh lemon juice*
  1/2 *teaspoon (2 mL) vanilla*

About 5 dozen cookies

In large mixing bowl, combine butter, granulated sugar, brown sugar, egg, 1 teaspoon (5 mL) peel, 1 tablespoon (15 mL) juice and 1 teaspoon (5 mL) vanilla. Beat at medium speed of electric mixer until light and fluffy. Add flour, baking soda and salt. Beat at low speed until soft dough forms. Cover with plastic wrap. Chill 1 to 2 hours, or until firm.

Heat oven to 400°F (200°C). Place dough in cookie press. Using flower-patterned plate, press cookies 2 inches (5 cm) apart onto ungreased cookie sheets. Bake for 5 to 7 minutes, or until edges are light golden brown. Cool completely.

In small mixing bowl, combine frosting ingredients. Beat at low speed of electric mixer until smooth. Spread frosting evenly on cookies. Let dry completely before storing.

Fattigmands

Vegetable oil
3 *tablespoons (50 mL) sour cream*
3 *tablespoons (50 mL) granulated sugar*
3 *egg yolks*
1/2 *teaspoon (2 mL) almond extract*
1/4 *teaspoon (1 mL) ground cloves*
1/4 *teaspoon (1 mL) salt*
1 1/4 *cups (300 mL) all-purpose flour, divided*
Powdered sugar

About 1 1/2 dozen cookies

In deep-fat fryer, heat 3 inches (8 cm) vegetable oil to 375°F (190°C). In small mixing bowl, combine sour cream, granulated sugar, egg yolks, almond extract, cloves and salt. Beat at medium speed of electric mixer until smooth. Add 1 cup (250 mL) flour. Beat at low speed until soft dough forms. Knead in enough of remaining 1/4 cup (50 mL) flour to form stiff dough.

On lightly floured surface, roll dough into 1/16 to 1/8-inch-thick (1.5 to 3 mm) rectangle. Using pastry wheel or sharp knife, cut dough into 2-inch (5 cm) strips. Cut strips diagonally at 4-inch (10 cm) intervals to form diamonds.

Cut 1-inch (2.5 cm) slit in center of each diamond. Pull one end of diamond completely through slit.

In hot oil, fry diamonds for 30 to 40 seconds, or until golden brown, turning over once. Drain on paper-towel-lined plate. Before serving, sprinkle fattigmands with powdered sugar.

Madeleines

2 *eggs*
Pinch of salt
1/2 *cup (125 mL) sugar*
1 *teaspoon (5 mL) grated lemon peel*
1/2 *teaspoon (2 mL) vanilla*
1/2 *cup (125 mL) plus 2 tablespoons (25 mL) all-purpose flour*
1/2 *cup (125 mL) butter or margarine, melted*

2 dozen cookies

Heat oven to 400°F (200°C). Heavily grease 12-form madeleine pan. Set aside. In medium mixing bowl, combine eggs and salt. Beat at high speed of electric mixer until foamy. Add sugar, peel and vanilla. Beat at high speed for 10 to 12 minutes, or until light and airy, scraping sides of bowl frequently. Using whisk, gently fold in flour, 2 tablespoons (25 mL) at a time. Gently fold in butter, 1 tablespoon (15 mL) at a time.

Spoon 1 measuring tablespoon (15 mL) batter into each madeleine form. Bake for 5 to 7 minutes, or until edges are golden brown. Let cool for 3 minutes before removing from pan. Carefully remove madeleines from pan. Cool flat-sides-down on wire racks.

Holiday & Special-occasion Cookies

Rosettes (bottom)

Vegetable oil
1 cup (250 mL) *whipping cream*
2 *eggs*
1 tablespoon (15 mL) *granulated sugar*
1 teaspoon (5 mL) *vanilla*
1/2 teaspoon (2 mL) *ground cinnamon*
1/2 teaspoon (2 mL) *salt*
3/4 cup (175 mL) *all-purpose flour*
Powdered sugar

About 4½ dozen cookies

In deep-fat fryer, heat 3 inches (8 cm) vegetable oil to 375°F (190°C). In medium mixing bowl, combine whipping cream, eggs, granulated sugar, vanilla, cinnamon and salt. Beat at low speed of electric mixer until smooth. Add flour. Beat at low speed until smooth.

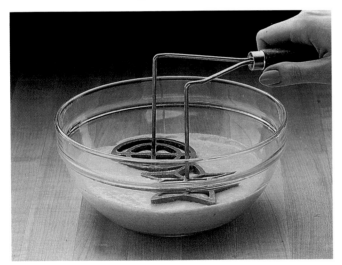

Heat rosette iron forms in hot oil for 30 seconds. Shake excess oil from forms. Dip hot forms into batter, making sure batter does not coat top side of forms. Immerse forms completely in hot oil. Fry for 25 to 35 seconds, or until golden brown. (Rosettes may release from forms. If so, remove from oil with slotted spoon.)

Drain on paper-towel-lined plate. Repeat with remaining batter. Before serving, sprinkle rosettes with powdered sugar.

Tips: If batter does not adhere to forms, batter may be too thin (add additional flour, 1 table-spoon/15 mL at a time), or oil may be too hot or too cold. If rosettes adhere to forms after they are browned, rap top of forms gently with knife handle. If batter begins to thicken, thin with small amount of whipping cream.

Chocolate Almond Rosettes (top)

Vegetable oil
1 cup (250 mL) *all-purpose flour*
1/4 cup (50 mL) *unsweetened cocoa*
3 tablespoons (50 mL) *granulated sugar*
1/2 teaspoon (2 mL) *salt*
1 cup (250 mL) *milk*
2 *eggs*
2 tablespoons (25 mL) *vegetable oil*
1/2 teaspoon (2 mL) *almond extract*
Powdered sugar

4 dozen cookies

In deep-fat fryer, heat 3 inches (8 cm) vegetable oil to 375°F (190°C). In medium mixing bowl, combine flour, cocoa, granulated sugar and salt. Add milk, eggs, oil and almond extract. Beat at medium speed of electric mixer until smooth.

Heat rosette iron forms in hot oil for 30 seconds. Shake excess oil from forms. Dip hot forms into batter, making sure batter does not coat top side of forms. Immerse forms completely in hot oil. Fry for 30 to 40 seconds, or until edges begin to brown. (Rosettes may release from forms. If so, remove from oil with slotted spoon.)

Drain on paper-towel-lined plate. Repeat with remaining batter. Before serving, sprinkle rosettes with powdered sugar.

Optional Glaze:

3 cups (750 mL) *powdered sugar*
3 to 4 tablespoons (50 mL) *milk*
1/2 teaspoon (2 mL) *almond extract*

In small bowl, combine glaze ingredients. Stir until smooth. Dip tops of cooled rosettes into glaze.

Orange-spiced Krumkake

1 cup (250 mL) sugar
1/2 cup (125 mL) butter or margarine, softened
2 eggs
1 teaspoon (5 mL) grated orange peel
1/4 teaspoon (1 mL) ground cloves
1/4 teaspoon (1 mL) ground cardamom
1 1/2 cups (375 mL) all-purpose flour
1 cup (250 mL) milk

5 dozen cookies

In medium mixing bowl, combine sugar, butter, eggs, peel, cloves and cardamom. Beat at medium speed of electric mixer until smooth. Gradually add flour, alternating with milk, beating at low speed until smooth batter forms, scraping sides of bowl frequently.

Brush inside of krumkake iron with small amount of vegetable shortening. Heat iron over medium-low heat (if using gas stove) or medium heat (if using electric stove).

Place 1 measuring tablespoon (15 mL) batter in center of open iron. Close iron and firmly hold together. Cook for 5 to 20 seconds, or until light golden brown, turning iron over once. (Watch carefully to prevent burning.)

Remove krumkake with spatula, and immediately roll into cone. Repeat with remaining batter. (The krumkake iron does not need to be rebrushed with shortening after the first krumkake is made.)

Holiday & Special-occasion Cookies

Pizzelles

2 cups (500 mL) all-purpose
   flour
1 cup (250 mL) sugar
4 eggs
3/4 cup (175 mL) butter or
   margarine, melted and
   slightly cooled
1/4 cup (50 mL) finely ground
   hazelnuts
1 tablespoon (15 mL) anise
   extract

About 3 1/2 dozen cookies

In medium mixing bowl, combine all ingredients. Beat at low speed of electric mixer until smooth batter forms, scraping sides of bowl frequently.

Brush inside of pizzelle iron with small amount of vegetable shortening. Heat iron over medium heat (if using gas stove) or medium-high heat (if using electric stove).

Place 1 measuring tablespoon (15 mL) batter in center of open iron. Close iron. (Do not squeeze shut.) Cook for 30 seconds to 1 minute 30 seconds, or until light golden brown, turning iron over once. (Watch carefully to prevent burning.)

With spatula, immediately remove pizzelle. Repeat with remaining batter. (The pizzelle iron does not need to be rebrushed with shortening after the first pizzelle is made.)

Cool pizzelles completely before storing. If desired, trim edges of cooled pizzelles with scissors.

Tip: To recrisp pizzelles, bake at 250°F (120°C) for 3 to 5 minutes.

Holiday & Special-occasion Cookies

Orange Snowballs

2³/₄ cups (675 mL) finely
      crushed vanilla wafers
  1 cup (250 mL) powdered
      sugar
  1 cup (250 mL) finely chopped
      almonds
¹/₃ cup (75 mL) butter or
      margarine, melted
¹/₄ cup (50 mL) frozen orange
      juice concentrate, defrosted
      Flaked coconut

            3¹/₂ dozen cookies

Line airtight container with
wax paper. Set aside. In large
mixing bowl, combine wafers,
sugar, almonds, butter and
concentrate. Stir until well
blended (mixture will be
crumbly).

Shape mixture into ³/₄-inch
(2 cm) balls. Roll balls in
coconut. Place balls in prepared container. Store in
refrigerator.

Choco-Brandy Balls

2¹/2 cups (625 mL) finely
        crushed chocolate wafers,
        divided
1¹/4 cups (300 mL) granulated
        sugar
  ¹/2 cup (125 mL) butter or
        margarine, melted
  ¹/2 cup (125 mL) finely chopped
        pecans
  ¹/4 cup (50 mL) brandy
        Powdered sugar

2¹/2 dozen cookies

Line airtight container with
wax paper. Set aside. In large
mixing bowl, combine 2 cups
(500 mL) wafers, the granulated
sugar, butter, pecans, and brandy. Stir until well blended (mixture will be crumbly).

Shape mixture into 1-inch
(2.5 cm) balls. Roll balls in remaining ¹/2 cup (125 mL)
wafers or powdered sugar.
Place balls in prepared container. Store in refrigerator.

Chocolate-Ginger Rocking Horse

2¹/₄ cups (550 mL) all-purpose flour
  ³/₄ cup (175 mL) unsweetened cocoa
   1 teaspoon (5 mL) baking soda
   1 teaspoon (5 mL) ground ginger
  ¹/₂ teaspoon (2 mL) baking powder
  ¹/₂ teaspoon (2 mL) ground allspice
  ¹/₄ teaspoon (1 mL) ground cardamom
  ¹/₄ teaspoon (1 mL) salt
   1 cup (250 mL) sugar
  ¹/₂ cup (125 mL) butter or margarine, softened
  ¹/₂ cup (125 mL) light molasses
   1 egg
  ¹/₂ teaspoon (2 mL) vanilla
      Decorator Frosting (see page 246)

About 3 dozen cookies

In medium mixing bowl, combine flour, cocoa, baking soda, ginger, baking powder, allspice, cardamom and salt. Set aside.

In large mixing bowl, combine sugar, butter, molasses, egg and vanilla. Beat at medium speed of electric mixer until well blended. Add flour mixture. Beat at low speed until soft dough forms. Cover with plastic wrap. Chill 2 to 3 hours, or until firm.

Heat oven to 350°F (180°C). Lightly grease cookie sheets. Set aside. Divide dough in half. On lightly floured surface, roll half of dough to ¹/₈ to ¹/₄-inch (3 to 5 mm) thickness. Using 3¹/₂-inch (9 cm) rocking horse cookie cutter, cut shapes into dough.

Place shapes 2 inches (5 cm) apart on prepared cookie sheets. Repeat with remaining dough. Bake for 8 to 10 minutes, or until set. Cool completely. Prepare frosting as directed. Decorate cookies as desired. Let dry completely before storing.

Holiday & Special-occasion Cookies

Candy-filled Chocolate Wheels

1½ cups (375 mL) powdered
      sugar
  1 cup (250 mL) butter or
      margarine, softened
  1 egg
  1 teaspoon (5 mL) vanilla
2⅔ cups (650 mL) all-purpose
      flour
  ¼ teaspoon (1 mL) salt
  ¼ cup (50 mL) unsweetened
      cocoa
  1 tablespoon (15 mL) milk
  ¼ cup (50 mL) finely crushed
      fruit-flavored hard candies

4 dozen cookies

In large mixing bowl, combine sugar, butter, egg and vanilla. Beat at medium speed of electric mixer until light and fluffy. Add flour and salt. Beat at low speed until soft dough forms.

Divide dough in half. Add cocoa and milk to half of dough. Beat at low speed until well blended. Roll chocolate dough between 2 sheets of wax paper into 12 x 8-inch (30 x 20 cm) rectangle. Discard top sheet of wax paper. Set dough aside.

Stir crushed candies into remaining half dough. Shape candied dough into 12-inch-long (30 cm) log. Place log lengthwise on long edge of rectangle. Roll chocolate dough jelly roll style around log. (Peel off wax paper when rolling.) Pinch edge to seal. Wrap in plastic wrap or wax paper. Chill 1 to 2 hours, or until firm.

Heat oven to 375°F (190°C). Cut roll into ¼-inch (5 mm) slices. Place slices 2 inches (5 cm) apart on ungreased cookie sheets. Bake for 8 to 10 minutes, or until set. Let cool for 1 minute before removing from cookie sheets. Cool completely before storing.

Chocolate-dipped Hazelnut Biscotti (top)

  1 cup (250 mL) slivered almonds
1½ cups (375 mL) sugar
  ½ cup (125 mL) unsalted butter, softened
  2 tablespoons (25 mL) hazelnut liqueur
  3 eggs
3¾ cups (925 mL) all-purpose flour
  2 teaspoons (10 mL) baking powder
     Pinch of salt
  1 cup (250 mL) milk chocolate chips
  2 teaspoons (10 mL) vegetable shortening
  ½ cup (125 mL) finely chopped hazelnuts

3½ dozen cookies

Heat oven to 350°F (180°C). Lightly grease cookie sheets. Set aside. Place almonds in 8-inch (2 L) square baking pan. Bake for 10 to 12 minutes, or until light golden brown, stirring occasionally. Coarsely chop almonds. Set aside.

In large mixing bowl, combine sugar, butter and liqueur. Beat at medium speed of electric mixer until light and fluffy. Add eggs, one at a time, beating after each addition. Add flour, baking powder and salt. Beat at low speed until soft dough forms. Stir in almonds.

Divide dough into quarters. On lightly floured surface, shape each quarter into 2-inch-diameter (5 cm) log. Place logs 2 inches (5 cm) apart on prepared cookie sheet. Bake for 30 to 35 minutes, or until golden brown.

Immediately cut logs diagonally into ¾-inch (2 cm) slices. Place slices 1 inch (2.5 cm) apart on prepared cookie sheets. Bake for additional 10 to 15 minutes, or until dry and golden brown. Cool completely.

In 1-quart (1 L) saucepan, combine chips and shortening. Melt over low heat, stirring constantly. Remove from heat. Dip one end of each cookie diagonally into melted chocolate. Sprinkle hazelnuts evenly over dipped ends. Let dry completely before storing.

Stained Glass Cookies (bottom)

    1 cup (250 mL) sugar
    ½ cup (125 mL) butter or margarine, softened
    ⅓ cup (75 mL) vegetable shortening
    2 eggs
    1 teaspoon (5 mL) grated orange peel
    1 teaspoon (5 mL) vanilla
2¾ cups (675 mL) all-purpose flour
    1 teaspoon (5 mL) baking powder
    1 teaspoon (5 mL) salt
    5 rolls (.9 oz./22 g each) ring-shaped hard
       candies (assorted flavors)

4 dozen cookies

In large mixing bowl, combine sugar, butter and shortening. Beat at medium speed of electric mixer until light and fluffy. Add eggs, peel and vanilla. Beat at medium speed until well blended. Add flour, baking powder and salt. Beat at low speed until soft dough forms. Cover with plastic wrap. Chill 1 to 2 hours, or until firm.

Heat oven to 350°F (180°C). Line cookie sheets with foil. Set aside. Divide dough into thirds. On well-floured surface, roll one third dough to ¼-inch (5 mm) thickness. Using 3-inch (8 cm) cookie cutters, cut desired shapes into dough. Place shapes 2 inches (5 cm) apart on prepared cookie sheets.

Using smaller cookie cutters, straws or a sharp knife, cut desired shapes out of cookies on cookie sheets. (If cookies are to be hung as ornaments, make a small hole at the top of each cookie for string.) Repeat with remaining dough.

Place like-colored candies in small plastic bags. Coarsely crush candies by tapping each bag with back of large spoon. Fill cutout areas of cookies to the top with candies. Bake for 7 to 9 minutes, or until edges are light golden brown and candies are melted. Cool completely before removing from foil. Gently pull cookies off foil.

Viennese Kiss Cookies

1½ cups (375 mL) all-purpose flour
¾ cup (175 mL) butter or margarine, chilled and
    cut into 1-inch (2.5 cm) pieces
¼ cup (50 mL) sugar
3 tablespoons (50 mL) sour cream
1 teaspoon (5 mL) vanilla
24 chocolate kisses

2 dozen cookies

Heat oven to 350°F (180°C). Grease two 12-cup miniature muffin pans (1¾-inch/4.5 cm diameter). Set aside. In large mixing bowl, combine flour, butter and sugar. Beat at medium speed of electric mixer until mixture resembles coarse crumbs. Add sour cream and vanilla. Beat at low speed until soft dough forms.

Shape dough into 1-inch (2.5 cm) balls. Place 1 ball in each prepared muffin cup. Bake for 20 to 25 minutes, or until edges are golden brown. Immediately press kiss into center of each cookie. Let cool for 1 minute before removing from pans. Cool completely before storing.

Poppy-Raspberry Kolachkes

1/2 cup (125 mL) butter or margarine, softened
 1 pkg. (3 oz./85 g) cream cheese, softened
1/4 cup (50 mL) granulated sugar
1/2 teaspoon (2 mL) vanilla
1 1/2 cups (375 mL) all-purpose flour
1 1/2 teaspoons (7 mL) poppy seed
1/3 cup (75 mL) raspberry jam

Glaze:

1/2 cup (125 mL) powdered sugar
 4 to 5 teaspoons (20 to 25 mL) half-and-half
1/4 teaspoon (1 mL) almond extract

About 3 dozen cookies

Heat oven to 375°F (190°C). In large mixing bowl, combine butter, cream cheese, granulated sugar and vanilla. Beat at medium speed of electric mixer until light and fluffy. Add flour and poppy seed. Beat at low speed until soft dough forms. Divide dough in half. On lightly floured board, roll half of dough to 1/8 to 1/4-inch (3 to 5 mm) thickness. Using 2 1/2-inch (6 cm) round cookie cutter, cut circles into dough. Place circles 2 inches (5 cm) apart on ungreased cookie sheets.

Spoon about 1/4 teaspoon (1 mL) raspberry jam onto center of each circle. Fold top half of circle over bottom half. Press edges with fork dipped in flour to seal. Repeat with remaining dough and jam. Bake for 7 to 9 minutes, or until edges are light golden brown. Cool completely.

In small mixing bowl, combine glaze ingredients. Stir until smooth. Drizzle glaze over cookies. Let dry completely before storing.

Fruitful Florentines

½ cup (125 mL) butter or
    margarine, softened
⅓ cup (75 mL) honey
¼ cup (50 mL) sugar
½ teaspoon (2 mL) vanilla
1 cup (250 mL) uncooked
    quick-cooking oats
⅔ cup (150 mL) all-purpose
    flour
1 cup (250 mL) chopped
    candied fruit

Glaze:
¼ cup (50 mL) semisweet
    chocolate chips
2 tablespoons (25 mL) butter
    or margarine

2½ dozen cookies

Heat oven to 350°F (180°C). Lightly grease cookie sheets. Set aside. In large mixing bowl, combine ½ cup (125 mL) butter, the honey, sugar and vanilla. Beat at medium speed of electric mixer until well blended. Add oats and flour. Beat at low speed until soft dough forms. Stir in candied fruit.

Drop dough by heaping teaspoons 2 inches (5 cm) apart onto prepared cookie sheets. Flatten dough slightly with back of spoon. Bake for 10 to 12 minutes, or until edges are golden brown. Let cool for 2 minutes before removing from cookie sheets. Cool completely.

In 1-quart (1 L) saucepan, combine glaze ingredients. Melt over low heat, stirring constantly. Drizzle glaze over cookies. Let dry completely before storing. Store in refrigerator.

Microwave tip: In small mixing bowl, melt glaze ingredients at 50% (Medium) for 2 to 4 minutes, stirring after every minute. Continue as directed.

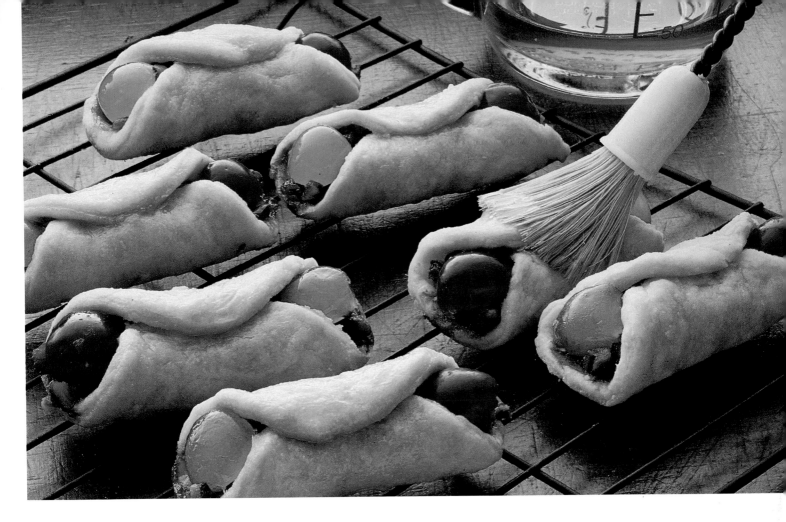

Greek Amaretto Cookies

2 tablespoons (25 mL) honey
1 tablespoon (15 mL) plus ¹/₂
   teaspoon (2 mL) amaretto,
   divided
1 jar (6 oz./170 g) red
   maraschino cherries, drained
   (reserve juice)
1 jar (6 oz./170 g) green
   maraschino cherries, drained
³/₄ cup (175 mL) chopped pecans
2 tablespoons (25 mL)
   strawberry jelly
2 cups (500 mL) all-purpose
   flour
¹/₄ teaspoon (1 mL) salt
³/₄ cup (175 mL) butter or
   margarine, chilled, cut into
   small pieces
5 to 6 tablespoons (75 to 90 mL)
   ice water

              2 dozen cookies

Heat oven to 400°F (200°C).
Lightly grease cookie sheets.
Set aside. In 1-cup (250 mL)
measure, combine honey and

2 teaspoons (10 mL) amaretto.
Set glaze aside.

Cut 12 red and 12 green cherries in half. Set aside. Chop remaining cherries. In medium
mixing bowl, combine re-
maining 1¹/₂ teaspoons (7 mL)
amaretto, the chopped cherries, reserved red cherry juice,
pecans and jelly. Set cherry
mixture aside.

In large mixing bowl, combine
flour and salt. Using pastry
blender, cut in butter until
mixture resembles coarse
crumbs. Sprinkle with water,
1 tablespoon (15 mL) at a time,
mixing with fork until par-
ticles are moistened and cling
together. Form dough into
ball. Divide dough in half.
Wrap half of dough in plastic
wrap. Chill.

On lightly floured surface, roll
remaining dough to ¹/₈-inch
(3 mm) thickness. Using 3-inch
(8 cm) round cookie cutter, cut
circles into dough.

Place heaping measuring teaspoon (5 mL) cherry mixture
onto center of each circle. Overlap two opposite sides to form
cylinders. Brush edges with
water. Press edges to seal.

Place cylinders 2 inches (5 cm)
apart on prepared cookie sheets.
Repeat with remaining dough
and cherry mixture. Insert 1 red
and 1 green cherry half into
opposite ends of each cylinder.
Bake for 17 to 19 minutes, or
until light golden brown. Immediately brush half of honey
glaze over top and sides of
cookies. Cool completely.
Brush remaining glaze over
cookies. Let dry completely
before storing.

Holiday & Special-occasion Cookies

Rum Balls

2 cups (500 mL) finely crushed vanilla wafers
1 cup (250 mL) granulated sugar
½ cup (125 mL) finely chopped walnuts
⅓ cup (75 mL) butter or margarine, melted
¼ cup (50 mL) light rum
 Powdered sugar

2½ dozen cookies

Line airtight container with wax paper. Set aside. In large mixing bowl, combine wafers, granulated sugar and walnuts. Add butter and rum. Stir until well blended (mixture will be crumbly).

Shape mixture into 1-inch (2.5 cm) balls. Roll balls in powdered sugar. Place on ungreased cookie sheets. Let stand for 1 hour. Reroll balls in powdered sugar before placing in prepared container. Store in refrigerator.

Tip: Flavor of rum balls improves after a few weeks' storage.

Chocolate Snowballs

2½ cups (625 mL) all-purpose flour
½ cup (125 mL) unsweetened cocoa
2 teaspoons (10 mL) baking powder
  Pinch of salt
3 cups (750 mL) sugar, divided
4 eggs
½ cup (125 mL) vegetable shortening
4 teaspoons (20 mL) vanilla, divided
  Granulated sugar
5 to 6 cups (1.25 to 1.5 L) flaked coconut
3 or 4 drops red food coloring
3 envelopes (.25 oz./7 g each) unflavored gelatin
⅔ cup (150 mL) ice water
1⅓ cups (325 mL) light corn syrup

8 dozen cookies

In medium mixing bowl, combine flour, cocoa, baking powder and salt. Set aside. In large mixing bowl, combine 2 cups (500 mL) sugar, the eggs, shortening and 2 teaspoons (10 mL) vanilla. Beat at medium speed of electric mixer until creamy. Add flour mixture. Beat at low speed until soft dough forms. Cover with plastic wrap. Chill 1 to 2 hours, or until firm.

Heat oven to 350°F (180°C). Lightly grease cookie sheets. Set aside. Shape dough into ½-inch (1 cm) balls. Place balls 2 inches (5 cm) apart on prepared cookie sheets. Flatten balls to 2-inch-diameter (5 cm) circles with bottom of drinking glass, dipping glass in granulated sugar to prevent sticking. Bake for 12 to 15 minutes, or until set. Cool completely.

Place coconut and food coloring in 1-gallon (4 L) sealable freezer bag. Shake to coat. Set aside. In top of double boiler, combine gelatin and ice water. Stir until gelatin is dissolved. Add remaining 1 cup (250 mL) sugar. In bottom of double boiler, bring additional water to boil. Place top of double boiler over boiling water. Cook gelatin mixture over medium heat until sugar is dissolved, stirring occasionally. Remove from heat.

In large mixing bowl, combine gelatin mixture, corn syrup and remaining 2 teaspoons (10 mL) vanilla. Beat at high speed of electric mixer for 15 minutes, or until topping is light and fluffy. Spoon about 1 tablespoon (15 mL) topping onto back of each cookie. Sprinkle topping with colored coconut. Let dry completely before storing.

Tip: Chocolate cookie can be made in advance and frozen in airtight container.

Apricot-Date Balls (top)

3/4 cup (175 mL) sugar
1/2 cup (125 mL) chopped dried apricots
1/2 cup (125 mL) chopped dates
2 eggs, beaten
1 cup (250 mL) finely chopped walnuts
1 teaspoon (5 mL) vanilla
Granulated sugar

4 dozen cookies

Line airtight container with wax paper. Set aside. In 2-quart (2 L) saucepan, combine 3/4 cup (175 mL) sugar, the apricots, dates and eggs. Cook over low heat for 6 to 8 minutes, or until mixture pulls away from side of pan, stirring constantly.

Remove from heat. Stir in walnuts and vanilla. Let stand for 45 to 50 minutes, or until mixture is cool enough to handle.

Shape mixture into 1-inch (2.5 cm) balls. Roll balls in sugar. Place balls in prepared container. Store in refrigerator.

Spicy Greek Jewels (bottom)

2 cups (500 mL) powdered sugar
1 cup (250 mL) butter or margarine, softened
1 egg
2 1/2 cups (625 mL) all-purpose flour
1 1/2 cups (375 mL) ground almonds
1 1/2 teaspoons (7 mL) apple pie spice
1/4 teaspoon (1 mL) salt
Powdered sugar
24 red candied cherries, halved
12 green candied pineapple chunks, each cut into 8 pieces

4 dozen cookies

Heat oven to 350°F (180°C). In large mixing bowl, combine 2 cups (500 mL) powdered sugar, the butter and egg. Beat at medium speed of electric mixer until light and fluffy. Add flour, almonds, apple pie spice and salt. Beat at low speed until soft dough forms.

Shape dough into 1-inch (2.5 cm) balls. Place balls 2 inches (5 cm) apart on ungreased cookie sheets. Flatten to 1/4-inch (5 mm) thickness with bottom of drinking glass, dipping glass in powdered sugar to prevent sticking.

Decorate each cookie with 1 cherry half and 2 pineapple pieces, pressing fruit lightly into dough. Bake for 12 to 14 minutes, or until edges are golden brown. Cool completely before storing.

French Lace Cookie Cups

1 cup (250 mL) all-purpose flour
1 cup (250 mL) finely chopped
   almonds
¹/₂ cup (125 mL) packed brown
   sugar
¹/₂ cup (125 mL) butter or
   margarine
¹/₃ cup (75 mL) light corn syrup
¹/₂ teaspoon (2 mL) almond extract

4 dozen cookies

Heat oven to 350°F (180°C).
Lightly grease cookie sheets
and outsides of 4 inverted 6-oz.
(175 mL) custard cups. Set aside.
In medium mixing bowl, combine
flour and almonds. Set aside.

In 1-quart (1 L) saucepan,
combine sugar, butter and
corn syrup. Bring to boil over
medium heat, stirring constantly. Remove from heat.
Gradually stir in flour mixture. Stir in extract.

Drop batter by measuring
tablespoons (15 mL) onto prepared cookie sheets, spreading
batter into 4-inch (10 cm) circles
(4 circles per sheet). Bake for
5 to 6 minutes, or until edges
are golden brown. Let cool for
1 minute before removing from
cookie sheets.

Place cookies over inverted
custard cups, molding around
cups and pinching edges to
shape. Let cookie cups cool
before removing from custard
cups. To serve, fill cookie cups
with cut-up fruit or ice cream.

Holiday & Special-occasion Cookies

Mexican Biscochitas

3 cups (750 mL) all-purpose flour
1 1/2 teaspoons (7 mL) baking powder
1/4 teaspoon (1 mL) salt
1 cup (250 mL) sugar, divided
1 cup (250 mL) vegetable shortening
1 egg
1 tablespoon (15 mL) anise seed
1/4 cup (50 mL) brandy
1 teaspoon (5 mL) ground cinnamon

About 4 dozen cookies

Heat oven to 350°F (180°C). In medium mixing bowl, combine flour, baking powder and salt. Set aside. In large mixing bowl, combine 3/4 cup (175 mL) sugar, the shortening, egg and anise seed. Beat at medium speed of electric mixer until light and fluffy. Gradually add flour mixture, alternating with brandy, beating at low speed until soft dough forms.

On lightly floured surface, roll dough to 1/4 to 1/2-inch (5 mm to 1 cm) thickness. Using 2 1/2-inch (6 cm) flower-shaped or round cookie cutter, cut shapes into dough. Place shapes 2 inches (5 cm) apart on ungreased cookie sheets. Set aside.

In small bowl, combine remaining 1/4 cup (50 mL) sugar and the cinnamon. Sprinkle shapes evenly with sugar mixture. Bake for 9 to 11 minutes, or until light golden brown. Cool completely before storing.

Greek Holiday Cookies

> 1 cup (250 mL) butter or margarine, softened
> 1/2 cup (125 mL) granulated sugar
> 1 egg
> 1/2 teaspoon (2 mL) vanilla
> 1/2 teaspoon (2 mL) brandy extract
> 2 1/2 cups (625 mL) all-purpose flour
> 1 teaspoon (5 mL) baking powder
> 1/4 teaspoon (1 mL) ground cloves
> 1/4 teaspoon (1 mL) salt
> Whole cloves
> Powdered sugar

4 1/2 dozen cookies

Heat oven to 350°F (180°C). In large mixing bowl, combine butter, granulated sugar, egg, vanilla and brandy extract. Beat at medium speed of electric mixer until light and fluffy. Add flour, baking powder, ground cloves and salt. Beat at low speed until soft dough forms.

Shape heaping teaspoons dough into crescent or S shapes. Place shapes 2 inches (5 cm) apart on ungreased cookie sheets. Press 2 whole cloves into each shape.

Bake for 9 to 11 minutes, or until set. Let cool for 1 minute before removing from cookie sheets. Sprinkle cookies with powdered sugar. Cool completely before storing. Remove whole cloves before eating.

Tip: Flavor of cookies improves after a few days' storage.

Chocolate-dipped Palmiers

1 pkg. (1 lb./454 g) frozen puff
   pastry dough, defrosted,
   divided
1/2 cup (125 mL) sugar
2 cups (500 mL) semisweet
   chocolate chips
3 teaspoons (15 mL) vegetable
   shortening, divided
1 1/2 cups (375 mL) vanilla
   baking chips

         6 dozen cookies

Heat oven to 375 °F (190°C).
Lightly grease cookie sheets.
Set aside. On lightly sugared
surface, roll 1 sheet pastry
into 12 x 10-inch (30 x 25 cm)
rectangle.

Fold long sides of pastry
toward center line, leaving 1/4-
inch (5 mm) gap in center. Fold
pastry in half lengthwise to
form 12 x 2 1/2-inch (30 x 6 cm)
strip. Lightly press edges
together to seal.

Cut dough crosswise into 1/4-
inch (5 mm) slices. Dip slices

in sugar. Place slices 2 inches
(5 cm) apart on prepared cookie
sheets. Bake for 8 to 10 minutes,
or until light golden brown,
rotating cookie sheet after 5
minutes. Repeat with remaining pastry. Cool completely.

In 1-quart (1 L) saucepan,
combine chocolate chips and
2 teaspoons (10 mL) shortening. Melt over low heat, stirring constantly. Repeat with
vanilla chips and remaining
1 teaspoon (5 mL) shortening.
Dip one end of each palmier
in melted chocolate. Let dry
on cooling rack. Dip again in
melted vanilla chips. Let dry
completely before storing.

Three-cornered Hats

1½ cups (375 mL) butter or
    margarine, softened
½ cup (125 mL) sugar
1 egg
¼ cup (50 mL) evaporated milk
½ teaspoon (2 mL) vanilla
2¾ cups (675 mL) all-purpose
    flour, divided

Filling:

1 pkg. (12 oz./341 g) pitted
    dried prunes
½ cup (125 mL) finely chopped
    walnuts
2 tablespoons (25 mL) sugar
1 to 2 teaspoons (5 to 10 mL)
    grated orange peel

1 egg yolk beaten with
    1 tablespoon (15 mL) water
      About 3 dozen cookies

In large mixing bowl, combine butter, ½ cup (125 mL) sugar and the egg. Beat at medium speed of electric mixer until light and fluffy. Add milk and vanilla. Beat at medium speed until well blended. Add 1¾ cups (425 mL) flour. Beat at low speed until soft dough forms. Stir in remaining 1 cup (250 mL) flour to form stiff dough. Cover with plastic wrap. Chill 30 minutes to 1 hour, or until firm.

In food processor or blender, process prunes until smooth. In medium mixing bowl, combine processed prunes and remaining filling ingredients. Set aside.

Heat oven to 350°F (180°C). Lightly grease cookie sheets. Set aside. On lightly floured surface, roll dough to ⅛ to ¼-inch (3 to 5 mm) thickness. Using 3-inch (8 cm) round cookie cutter, cut circles into dough. Place circles 2 inches (5 cm) apart on prepared cookie sheets.

Place heaping measuring teaspoon (5 mL) filling onto center of each circle. Lightly brush edges with water. Bring sides of dough up and pinch together to form triangle, leaving top of triangle open to show filling. Lightly brush top and sides of dough with egg yolk mixture. Bake for 14 to 16 minutes, or until set. Cool completely before storing.

Holiday & Special-occasion Cookies

German Pfeffernüsse

1 cup (250 mL) granulated
   sugar
3/4 cup (175 mL) butter or
   margarine, softened
1 cup (250 mL) dark corn
   syrup
3 tablespoons (50 mL) hot
   water
2 teaspoons (10 mL) anise seed
1 teaspoon (5 mL) black pepper
1 teaspoon (5 mL) baking soda
1/4 teaspoon (1 mL) ground
   allspice
1/4 teaspoon (1 mL) ground
   cardamom
1/4 teaspoon (1 mL) ground
   cloves
1/4 teaspoon (1 mL) salt
4 to 5 cups (1 to 1.25 L)
   all-purpose flour, divided
   Powdered sugar

About 9 dozen cookies

In large mixing bowl, combine granulated sugar and butter. Beat at medium speed of electric mixer until light and fluffy. Add corn syrup, water, anise, pepper, baking soda, allspice, cardamom, cloves and salt. Beat at low speed until well blended.

Gradually add 4 cups (1 L) flour, beating at low speed. Stir or knead in enough of remaining 1 cup (250 mL) flour to form stiff dough. Cover with plastic wrap. Chill 3 to 4 hours, or until firm.

Heat oven to 350°F (180°C). Divide dough into 8 pieces. Roll each piece into 1/2 to 3/4-inch-thick (1 to 2 cm) rope. Cut ropes diagonally into 1 to 1 1/2-inch (2.5 to 4 cm) lengths. Place lengths 2 inches (5 cm) apart on ungreased cookie sheets. Bake for 10 to 15 minutes, or until golden brown. Cool completely. Roll in powdered sugar before storing.

Orange-spiced Shortbread

2¼ cups (550 mL) all-purpose flour
 ⅔ cup (150 mL) sugar
  1 teaspoon (5 mL) grated orange peel
 ¼ to ½ teaspoon (1 to 2 mL) ground nutmeg
      Pinch of salt
1¼ cups (300 mL) butter, chilled, cut into small
      pieces

5⅓ dozen cookies

Heat oven to 325°F (160°C). Lightly grease two 8-inch (2 L) square baking pans. Set aside. In large mixing bowl, combine flour, sugar, peel, nutmeg and salt. Using pastry blender, cut in butter until mixture resembles coarse crumbs. Form dough into ball.

Divide dough in half. Press halves evenly into prepared pans. Using fork, prick dough at 1-inch (2.5 cm) intervals. Bake for 30 to 35 minutes, or until light golden brown. Immediately cut shortbread into 2-inch (5 cm) squares, then cut each square diagonally to form triangles. Cool completely in pans before storing.

Holiday & Special-occasion Cookies

Holiday Meringue Cookies

> 3 egg whites
> ½ teaspoon (2 mL) white vinegar
>   Pinch of salt
> 1¼ cups (300 mL) sugar
> ½ teaspoon (2 mL) vanilla
>   Any combination cinnamon candies, multicolored shot, chocolate-flavored candy sprinkles, etc.
>
>   About 1 dozen cookies

Heat oven to 300°F (150°C). Line cookie sheets with parchment paper. Set aside. In small mixing bowl, combine egg whites, vinegar and salt.

Beat at high speed of electric mixer until soft peaks form. Add sugar, 1 tablespoon (15 mL) at a time, beating at high speed. Beat until stiff peaks form. Beat in vanilla.

Fill pastry bag with meringue mixture. Using open star tip, pipe holiday designs 1 inch (2.5 cm) apart on prepared cookie sheets. Decorate as desired with candies, shot, sprinkles, etc.

Bake for 23 to 25 minutes, or until light golden brown. Cool completely before removing from parchment paper.

Butter Cookie Wreaths

 8 oz. (250 g) white or chocolate-
      flavored candy coating
 1 teaspoon (5 mL) vegetable
      shortening
36 butter cookies (2-inch/5 cm)
      with hole in center
      Red or green colored sugar
      Red cinnamon candies
36 pieces shoestring licorice
      (4-inch/10 cm lengths)

           3 dozen cookies

Line cookie sheets with wax paper. Set aside. In 1-quart (1 L) saucepan, combine candy coating and shortening. Melt over low heat, stirring constantly. Dip top of each cookie into coating. Place cookies dipped-sides-up on prepared cookie sheets. Decorate each cookie with colored sugar and cinnamon candies. Tie licorice into bows. Use coating to attach bows to each cookie. Let dry completely before storing.

Christmas Jewel Kiss: Omit cinnamon candies and shoestring licorice. Place chocolate kiss in center of each dipped cookie. Continue as directed.

Microwave tip: In small mixing bowl, melt candy coating and shortening at 50% (Medium) for 2½ to 5 minutes, stirring after every minute. Continue as directed.

Holiday & Special-occasion Cookies

Ginger Man Sandwich Cookies

12 oz. (375 g) white candy
   coating
1½ teaspoons (7 mL) vegetable
   shortening
   Red or green food color
   paste (optional)
3 pkgs. (5 oz./142 g each)
   ginger man cookies
30 pieces shoestring licorice
   (4-inch/10 cm lengths)
   Red cinnamon candies

2½ dozen cookies

Line cookie sheets with wax paper. Set aside. In 1-quart (1 L) saucepan, combine candy coating and shortening. Melt over low heat, stirring constantly. Add food color paste. Mix well.

Spoon small amount of coating onto backs of half of cookies. Place cookies coated-sides-up on prepared cookie sheets. Fold licorice pieces in half to form loops. Place 1 loop at head end of each cookie, with cut ends in coating on cookie.

Gently press backs of remaining half of cookies against filling to form sandwiches. Decorate one side, using remaining coating to attach cinnamon candies for eyes, nose and buttons. Let dry completely before storing.

Microwave tip: In medium mixing bowl, melt candy coating and shortening at 50% (Medium) for 2½ to 5½ minutes, stirring after every minute. Continue as directed.

Snowman Macaroons (left)

8 oz. (250 g) white candy coating
1 teaspoon (5 mL) vegetable shortening
24 macaroon cookies (2-inch/5 cm)
   Flaked coconut
24 red cinnamon candies
24 raisins, cut in half
24 pieces red shoestring licorice (3/4-inch/2 cm
   lengths)
24 pieces black shoestring licorice (1/2-inch/1 cm
   lengths)
1/2 cup (125 mL) sugar, divided
48 large black gumdrops

2 dozen cookies

Line cookie sheets with wax paper. Set aside. In 1-quart (1 L) saucepan, combine candy coating and shortening. Melt over low heat, stirring constantly. Dip top of each cookie into coating. Place cookies dipped-sides-up on prepared cookie sheets.

Sprinkle each cookie with coconut. Use remaining coating to attach cinnamon candy for nose, raisin halves for eyes and red licorice for mouth. Use black licorice for stem of pipe.

For hat and bowl of pipe, sprinkle 1 teaspoon (5 mL) sugar on piece of wax paper. Place 2 large black gumdrops on sugar. Top with another piece of wax paper. Roll gumdrops between wax paper to 1/4-inch (5 mm) thickness. Cut flattened gumdrops into shape of hat and pipe bowl. Attach with coating. Repeat for remaining snowmen. Let dry completely before storing.

Microwave tip: In small mixing bowl, melt candy coating and shortening at 50% (Medium) for 2 1/2 to 5 minutes, stirring after every minute. Continue as directed.

Christmas Bear Cookies (right)

8 oz. (250 g) white candy coating
1 teaspoon (5 mL) vegetable shortening
24 macaroon cookies (2-inch/5 cm)
   Flaked coconut
24 red cinnamon candies
24 miniature marshmallows, flattened
48 miniature chocolate chips
12 large marshmallows, quartered
   Red colored sugar
24 large gumdrops, cut in half lengthwise
24 candy-coated plain chocolate pieces

2 dozen cookies

Line cookie sheets with wax paper. Set aside. In 1-quart (1 L) saucepan, combine candy coating and shortening. Melt over low heat, stirring constantly. Dip top of each cookie into coating. Place cookies dipped-sides-up on prepared cookie sheets.

Sprinkle each cookie with coconut. Use remaining coating to attach cinnamon candy to center of each flattened marshmallow and attach marshmallow to each cookie for nose. Attach chocolate chips for eyes and marshmallow quarter to each side of cookie for ears. Spread small amount of coating on each ear, and sprinkle with colored sugar.

Use coating to attach 2 gumdrop halves to make bow tie and to attach candy-coated chocolate piece in center of each bow. Let dry completely before storing.

Microwave tip: In small mixing bowl, melt candy coating and shortening at 50% (Medium) for 2 1/2 to 5 minutes, stirring after every minute. Continue as directed.

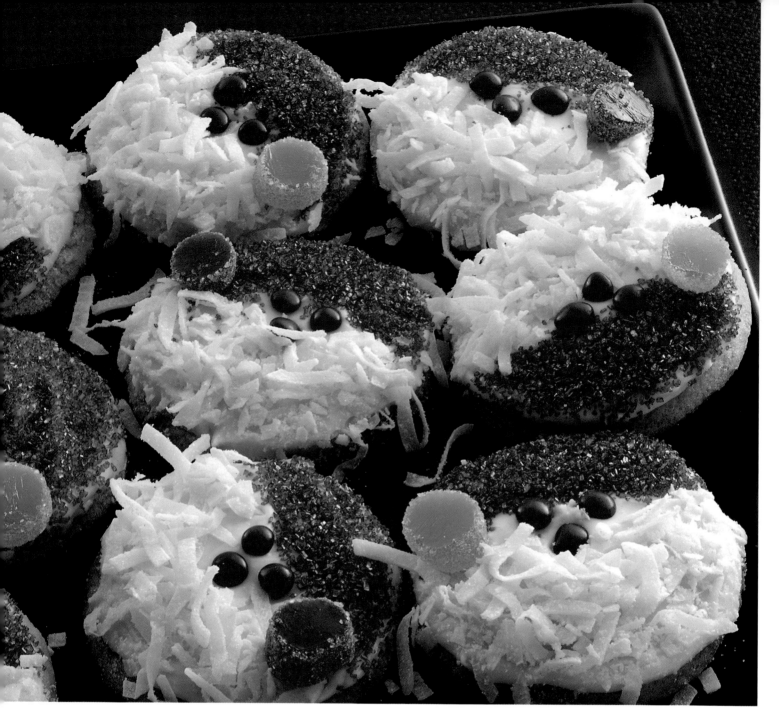

Santa Cookies

8 oz. (250 g) white or chocolate-
    flavored candy coating
1 teaspoon (5 mL) vegetable
    shortening
24 sugar cookies (2½-inch/6 cm)
    Red or green colored sugar
    Flaked coconut
12 small gumdrops, cut in
    half crosswise
72 red cinnamon candies

    2 dozen cookies

Line cookie sheets with wax paper. Set aside. In 1-quart (1 L) saucepan, combine candy coating and shortening. Melt over low heat, stirring constantly. Dip top of each cookie into coating. Place cookies dipped-sides-up on prepared cookie sheets.

Decorate each Santa with colored sugar to make hat, and coconut to make beard. Use gumdrop half to make pom-pom for hat, and cinnamon candies for eyes and nose. Let dry completely before storing.

Microwave tip: In small mixing bowl, melt candy coating and shortening at 50% (Medium) for 2½ to 5 minutes, stirring after every minute. Continue as directed.

Holiday & Special-occasion Cookies

Santa's Elf Cookies

  8 oz. (250 g) white candy coating
  1 teaspoon (5 mL) vegetable
     shortening
 24 sugar cookies (2½-inch/6 cm)
     Red or green colored sugar
 24 miniature marshmallows
 48 semisweet chocolate chips
 24 red cinnamon candies
 24 small red gumdrops, cut in
     half crosswise
 24 pieces red shoestring licorice
     (1-inch/2.5 cm lengths)

                    2 dozen cookies

Line cookie sheets with wax paper. Set aside. In 1-quart (1 L) saucepan, combine candy coating and shortening. Melt over low heat, stirring constantly. Dip half of each cookie into coating to make hat. Place cookies on prepared cookie sheets.

Decorate each elf with colored sugar to make hat. Use remaining coating to attach marshmallow for pom-pom of hat, and chocolate chips for eyes. Attach cinnamon candy for nose, gumdrop halves for cheeks and piece of licorice for mouth. Let dry completely before storing.

Microwave tip: In small mixing bowl, melt candy coating and shortening at 50% (Medium) for 2½ to 5 minutes, stirring after every minute. Continue as directed.

Holiday & Special-occasion Cookies

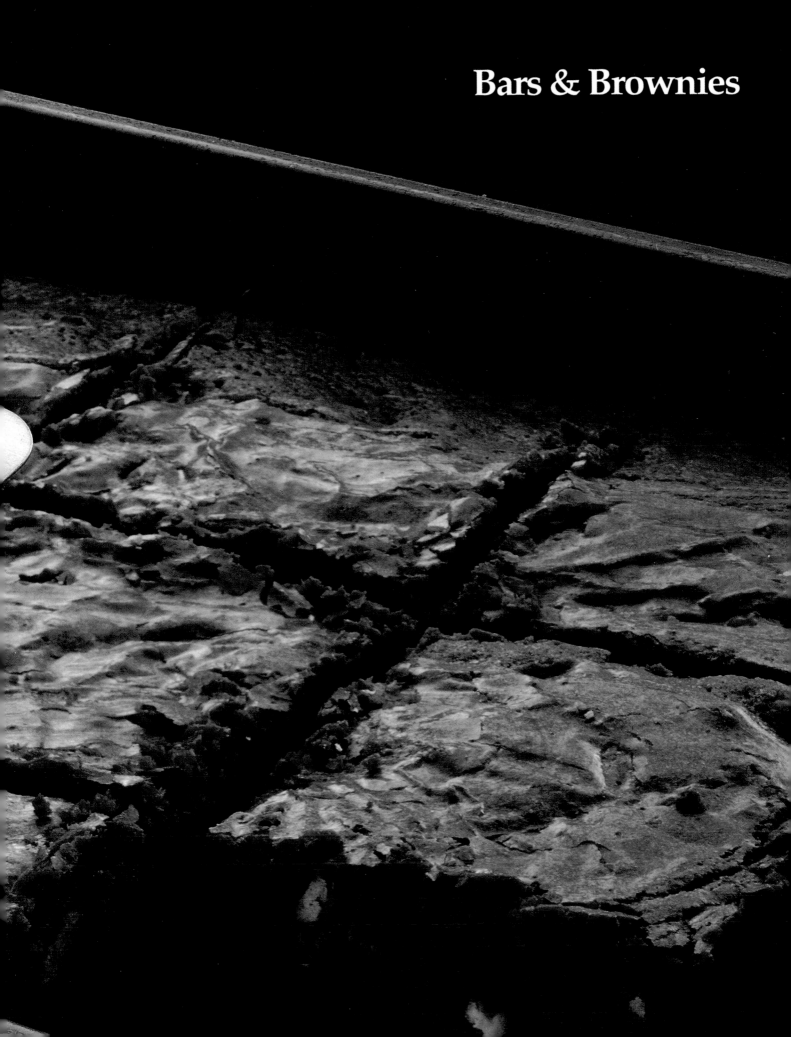

Bars & Brownies

Bar & Brownie Basics

When making bars and brownies, use the pan specifically called for in the recipe. If the pan is larger, the bars will be thinner and drier. If the pan is smaller, the bars will be thicker and may not bake completely.

Bars and brownies should be left in the pan to cool before cutting, unless the recipe directs otherwise. If desired, line the baking pan with foil for easy removal of the bars and quick cleanup (shown on opposite page).

Many bars and brownies can be stored in the baking pan if it is tightly covered with a lid or foil. Follow individual recipes for specific storage directions.

Standard Sizes of Baking Pans for Bars and Brownies

15½ x 10½ x 1-inch (40 x 25 x 2.5 cm) jelly roll pan

13 x 9-inch (3.5 L) pan with lid

8-inch (2 L) square pan

11 x 7-inch (2 L) pan

Doneness Tests for Bars and Brownies

Bars: Cakelike bars are done when a slight impression remains when the bars are lightly touched in the center, the edges begin to appear dry and pull away from the sides of the pan or when a wooden pick inserted near the center comes out clean.

Brownies: Most brownies are done when a wooden pick inserted in the center comes out with a moist crumb on it. Brownies also may pull away from the sides of the pan and the top may appear dry but shiny.

Tips for Bars and Brownies

Line the baking pan with foil and grease the foil before spreading the batter in the pan. When bars or brownies are ready to be cut, pull and lift the foil to remove bars from pan, and transfer them to a cutting board.

Use a ruler to cut bars and brownies evenly; mark where you will cut by scoring the surface with a knife. Cut bars into rectangles, squares, triangles or diamonds. To make triangles, cut bars into squares, then cut each square in half diagonally. Diamonds are made by cutting lengthwise parallel lines on the bars, about 1½ inches (4 cm) apart, and then making diagonal cuts across the straight lines, about 1½ inches (4 cm) apart.

Almond Pie Bars

> 2 cups (500 mL) all-purpose flour
> 1/2 cup (125 mL) powdered sugar
> 1 cup (250 mL) butter or margarine, chilled

Topping:

> 2 cups (500 mL) granulated sugar
> 1 cup (250 mL) chopped almonds
> 4 eggs, slightly beaten
> 1/2 cup (125 mL) butter or margarine, melted
> 1/3 cup (75 mL) light corn syrup
> 2 tablespoons (25 mL) all-purpose flour
> 1/2 teaspoon (2 mL) almond extract

32 bars

Heat oven to 350°F (180°C). In medium mixing bowl, combine 2 cups (500 mL) flour and the powdered sugar. Using pastry blender, cut in chilled butter until mixture resembles coarse crumbs.

Press flour mixture evenly into ungreased 13 x 9-inch (3.5 L) baking pan to form base. Bake for 10 to 15 minutes, or until edges are light golden brown.

In second medium mixing bowl, combine topping ingredients. Spread topping evenly over base. Bake for additional 25 to 28 minutes, or until deep golden brown. (Filling will set as it cools.) Cool completely before cutting. Store in refrigerator.

Peanut Butter Oat Bars

1 cup (250 mL) peanut butter chips

1 cup (250 mL) semisweet chocolate chips

3/4 cup (175 mL) butter or margarine, softened, divided

1 can (14 oz./396 g) sweetened condensed milk

1 1/2 cups (375 mL) all-purpose flour

1 cup (250 mL) uncooked quick-cooking oats

1 cup (250 mL) packed brown sugar

1 egg

1/2 teaspoon (2 mL) baking soda

1/2 teaspoon (2 mL) vanilla

3/4 cup (175 mL) chopped salted peanuts

32 bars

Heat oven to 350°F (180°C). Lightly grease 13 x 9-inch (3.5 L) baking pan. Set aside. In 1-quart (1 L) saucepan, combine chips and 1/4 cup (50 mL) butter. Melt over medium heat, stirring constantly. Remove from heat. Stir in milk. Set aside.

In large mixing bowl, combine remaining 1/2 cup (125 mL) butter, the flour, oats, sugar, egg, baking soda and vanilla. Stir until well blended. Reserve 1/2 cup (125 mL) flour mixture.

Press remaining flour mixture evenly into prepared pan to form base. Spread chip mixture evenly over base. Sprinkle reserved flour mixture and peanuts evenly over chip mixture. Bake for 20 to 30 minutes, or until golden brown. Cool completely before cutting.

Mile High Yogurt Brownies

1¼ cups (300 mL) sugar
  1 cup (250 mL) plain nonfat or low-fat yogurt
  3 eggs
 ½ cup (125 mL) butter or margarine, softened
  3 squares (1 oz./30 g each) unsweetened baking
     chocolate, melted and slightly cooled
  1 teaspoon (5 mL) vanilla
  1 cup (250 mL) all-purpose flour
 ½ teaspoon (2 mL) baking powder
 ¼ teaspoon (1 mL) baking soda
 ¼ teaspoon (1 mL) salt

Frosting:
  1 cup (250 mL) semisweet chocolate chips
 ¼ cup (50 mL) plain nonfat or low-fat yogurt

16 brownies

Heat oven to 350°F (180°C). Lightly grease and flour 8-inch (2 L) square baking pan. Set aside. In large mixing bowl, combine sugar, 1 cup (250 mL) yogurt, the eggs, butter, melted chocolate and vanilla. Beat at medium speed of electric mixer until well blended. Add flour, baking powder, baking soda and salt. Beat at low speed until well blended. Spread mixture evenly in prepared pan. Bake for 30 to 35 minutes, or until wooden pick inserted in center comes out clean. Cool completely.

In 1-quart (1 L) saucepan, melt chips over low heat, stirring constantly. Remove from heat. Add ¼ cup (50 mL) yogurt. Stir until smooth. Spread frosting evenly over brownies.

Orange Cream Prune Bars

Filling:

1½ cups (375 mL) sour cream
1½ cups (375 mL) chopped orange essence prunes
¾ cup (175 mL) packed brown sugar
3 egg yolks
1 tablespoon (15 mL) cornstarch
1 teaspoon (5 mL) grated orange peel
1 teaspoon (5 mL) vanilla

2 cups (500 mL) uncooked quick-cooking oats
1¼ cups (300 mL) all-purpose flour
¾ cup (175 mL) packed brown sugar
½ teaspoon (2 mL) baking soda
¾ cup (175 mL) butter or margarine, chilled

32 bars

Heat oven to 350°F (180°C). Lightly grease 13 x 9-inch (3.5 L) baking pan. Set aside. In 2-quart (2 L) saucepan, combine filling ingredients. Cook over medium heat until thickened, stirring constantly. Cool slightly. Set aside.

In medium mixing bowl, combine oats, flour, ¾ cup (175 mL) brown sugar and the baking soda. Using pastry blender, cut in butter until mixture resembles coarse crumbs. Reserve 1½ cups (375 mL) oat mixture.

Press remaining oat mixture evenly into prepared pan to form base. Bake for 10 minutes. Spread filling evenly over base. Sprinkle reserved oat mixture evenly over filling. Bake for additional 20 to 25 minutes, or until light golden brown. Cool completely before cutting.

Apricot Streusel Bars (top)

Filling:
 2 pkgs. (6 oz./170 g each) dried apricots, chopped
 3/4 cup (175 mL) sugar
 1/2 cup (125 mL) water

 2 cups (500 mL) all-purpose flour
 1/4 cup (50 mL) sugar
 1/2 teaspoon (2 mL) baking soda
 1/2 teaspoon (2 mL) salt
 1 cup (250 mL) butter or margarine, chilled
 1/2 cup (125 mL) flaked coconut
 1/2 cup (125 mL) uncooked quick-cooking oats
 1/2 cup (125 mL) chopped pecans

32 bars

Heat oven to 350°F (180°C). In 2-quart (2 L) saucepan, combine filling ingredients. Cook over medium heat until thickened, stirring constantly. Remove from heat. Set aside.

In medium mixing bowl, combine flour, 1/4 cup (50 mL) sugar, the baking soda and salt. Using pastry blender, cut in butter until mixture resembles coarse crumbs. Stir in coconut, oats and pecans. Reserve 1 1/2 cups (375 mL) flour mixture.

Press remaining flour mixture evenly into ungreased 13 x 9-inch (3.5 L) baking pan to form base. Bake for 10 to 12 minutes, or until edges are light golden brown.

Carefully spread filling evenly over base. Sprinkle reserved flour mixture evenly over filling. Bake for additional 20 to 30 minutes, or until light golden brown. Cool completely before cutting.

Frosted Zucchini Bars (bottom)

 3/4 cup (175 mL) butter or margarine, softened
 1/2 cup (125 mL) granulated sugar
 1/2 cup (125 mL) packed brown sugar
 2 eggs
 1 teaspoon (5 mL) grated orange peel
 1 teaspoon (5 mL) vanilla
 1 3/4 cups (425 mL) all-purpose flour
 1 teaspoon (5 mL) baking powder
 1/4 teaspoon (1 mL) salt
 2 cups (500 mL) grated zucchini
 1 cup (250 mL) golden raisins
 1/2 cup (125 mL) flaked coconut

Frosting:
 3 cups (750 mL) powdered sugar
 1/2 cup (125 mL) butter or margarine, softened
 1 pkg. (3 oz./85 g) cream cheese, softened
 1 teaspoon (5 mL) grated orange peel
 1 tablespoon (15 mL) fresh orange juice
 1/2 teaspoon (2 mL) vanilla

24 bars

Heat oven to 350°F (180°C). Lightly grease 13 x 9-inch (3.5 L) baking pan. Set aside. In large mixing bowl, combine 3/4 cup (175 mL) butter, the granulated sugar, brown sugar, eggs, 1 teaspoon (5 mL) peel and 1 teaspoon (5 mL) vanilla. Beat at medium speed of electric mixer until light and fluffy. Add flour, baking powder and salt. Beat at low speed until well blended. Stir in zucchini, raisins and coconut.

Spread mixture evenly in prepared pan. Bake for 20 to 25 minutes, or until slight impression remains when bars are lightly touched in center. Cool completely.

In medium mixing bowl, combine frosting ingredients. Beat at low speed of electric mixer until smooth. Spread frosting evenly over bars.

Candy-topped Brownies

1 cup (250 mL) sugar
½ cup (125 mL) butter or
   margarine, softened
1¼ cups (300 mL) chocolate-
   flavored syrup
3 eggs
2 teaspoons (10 mL) vanilla
1½ cups (375 mL) all-purpose
   flour
½ cup (125 mL) milk chocolate
   chips

Frosting:

⅓ cup (75 mL) butter or
   margarine
⅓ cup (75 mL) sugar
¼ cup (50 mL) milk
1 cup (250 mL) milk chocolate
   chips

1 cup (250 mL) candy-coated
   plain chocolate pieces

24 brownies

Heat oven to 350°F (180°C). Lightly grease 13 x 9-inch (3.5 L) baking pan. Set aside. In large mixing bowl, combine 1 cup (250 mL) sugar and ½ cup (125 mL) butter. Beat at medium speed of electric mixer until light and fluffy. Add syrup, eggs and vanilla. Beat at medium speed until well blended. Add flour. Beat at low speed until well blended. Stir in ½ cup (125 mL) chips.

Spread mixture evenly in prepared pan. Bake for 33 to 38 minutes, or until wooden pick inserted in center comes out clean. Cool completely.

In 1-quart (1 L) saucepan, combine ⅓ cup (75 mL) butter, ⅓ cup (75 mL) sugar and the milk. Bring to boil over medium heat, stirring frequently. Boil for 1 minute. Remove from heat. Add 1 cup (250 mL) chips. Stir until smooth. Spread frosting evenly over brownies. Sprinkle frosting evenly with chocolate pieces.

Bars & Brownies

Lime Squares

- 1 cup (250 mL) all-purpose flour
- 1/3 cup (75 mL) packed brown sugar
- 1/3 cup (75 mL) butter or margarine, chilled

Topping:

- 1 cup (250 mL) granulated sugar
- 2 eggs
- 2 teaspoons (10 mL) grated lime peel
- 2 tablespoons (25 mL) fresh lime juice
- 2 tablespoons (25 mL) all-purpose flour
- 1/2 teaspoon (2 mL) baking powder
- 1/4 teaspoon (1 mL) salt

  Powdered sugar

16 bars

Heat oven to 325°F (160°C). Lightly grease 8-inch (2 L) square baking pan. Set aside. In medium mixing bowl, combine 1 cup (250 mL) flour and the brown sugar. Using pastry blender, cut in butter until mixture resembles coarse crumbs. Press mixture evenly into prepared pan to form base. Bake for 10 minutes.

In second medium mixing bowl, combine topping ingredients. Beat at medium speed of electric mixer until well blended. Spread topping evenly over base. Bake for additional 18 to 20 minutes, or until edges are light golden brown. Cool completely. Sprinkle bars evenly with powdered sugar. Store in refrigerator.

Macadamia Vanilla Blondies

½ cup (125 mL) butter or
    margarine
4 squares (1 oz./30 g each)
    white baking chocolate
1 cup (250 mL) packed brown
    sugar
½ cup (125 mL) granulated
    sugar
2 teaspoons (10 mL) vanilla
4 eggs
2 cups (500 mL) all-purpose
    flour
½ teaspoon (2 mL) baking
    powder
¼ teaspoon (1 mL) salt
1 cup (250 mL) flaked coconut
½ cup (125 mL) chopped
    macadamia nuts
½ cup (125 mL) vanilla baking
    chips

24 brownies

Heat oven to 350°F (180°C).
Lightly grease 13 x 9-inch
(3.5 L) baking pan. Set aside.
In 3-quart (3 L) saucepan, combine butter and white chocolate. Melt over medium heat,
stirring constantly. Remove
from heat. Cool slightly.

Stir in sugars and vanilla.
Add eggs, one at a time, beating after each addition. Add
flour, baking powder and salt.
Stir until well blended. Stir in
coconut, nuts and chips.

Spread mixture evenly in prepared pan. Bake for 30 to 35
minutes, or until wooden pick
inserted in center comes out
clean. Cool completely before
cutting.

Chocolate Caramel Brownies

2 *cups (500 mL) granulated sugar*
1 *cup (250 mL) butter or margarine, softened*
1/2 *cup (125 mL) mashed banana (1 medium)*
2 *teaspoons (10 mL) vanilla*
4 *eggs*
1 1/2 *cups (375 mL) all-purpose flour*
3/4 *cup (175 mL) unsweetened cocoa*
1 *teaspoon (5 mL) baking powder*
1/2 *teaspoon (2 mL) salt*
1 *cup (250 mL) butterscotch chips*
1/2 *cup (125 mL) semisweet chocolate chips*

Frosting:
2 *tablespoons (25 mL) butter or margarine*
1/4 *cup (50 mL) unsweetened cocoa*
1 1/2 *cups (375 mL) powdered sugar*
1/4 *cup (50 mL) caramel ice cream topping*
1 *to 2 tablespoons (15 to 25 mL) milk*
1 *teaspoon (5 mL) vanilla*

2 *tablespoons (25 mL) caramel ice cream topping*
2 *teaspoons (10 mL) all-purpose flour*

32 brownies

Heat oven to 350°F (180°C). Lightly grease 13 x 9-inch (3.5 L) baking pan. Set aside. In large mixing bowl, combine granulated sugar and 1 cup (250 mL) butter. Beat at medium speed of electric mixer until light and fluffy. Add banana and 2 teaspoons (10 mL) vanilla. Beat at medium speed until well blended. Add eggs, one at a time, beating after each addition. Add 1 1/2 cups (375 mL) flour, 3/4 cup (175 mL) cocoa, the baking powder and salt. Beat at low speed until well blended. Stir in chips.

Spread mixture evenly in prepared pan. Bake for 30 to 40 minutes, or until wooden pick inserted in center comes out clean. Cool completely.

In 1-quart (1 L) saucepan, melt 2 tablespoons (25 mL) butter over medium heat. Add 1/4 cup (50 mL) cocoa. Cook over medium heat just until mixture comes to boil, stirring constantly. Remove from heat. Cool slightly. Add remaining frosting ingredients. Stir until smooth. Spread frosting evenly over brownies.

In small bowl, combine 2 tablespoons (25 mL) topping and 2 teaspoons (10 mL) flour. Stir until smooth. Drizzle over frosting.

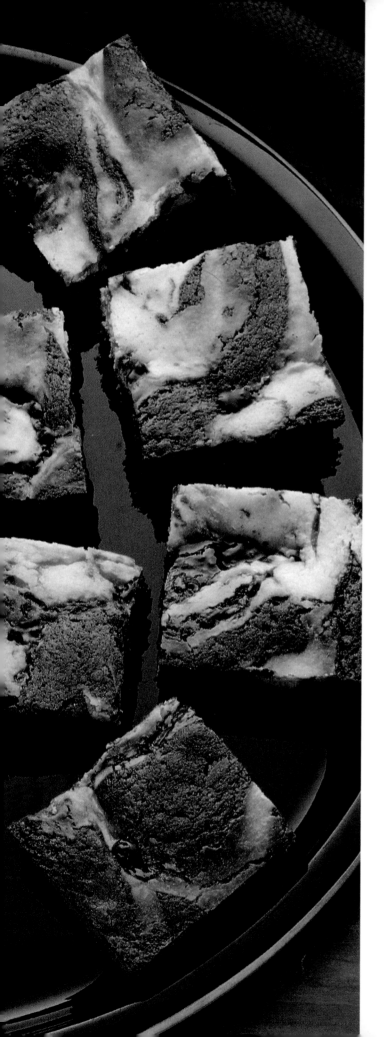

Raspberry Cream Cheese Brownies

1/2 cup (125 mL) butter or margarine
4 squares (1 oz./30 g each) unsweetened baking chocolate
2 cups (500 mL) sugar
2 tablespoons (25 mL) raspberry liqueur
4 eggs
1 cup (250 mL) all-purpose flour
1/2 teaspoon (2 mL) baking powder
1/2 teaspoon (2 mL) salt

Filling:

1 pkg. (8 oz./227 g) cream cheese, softened
1/3 cup (75 mL) sugar
1 egg
1/2 teaspoon (2 mL) vanilla

1/2 cup (125 mL) raspberry preserves

24 brownies

Heat oven to 350°F (180°C). Lightly grease 13 x 9-inch (3.5 L) baking pan. In 3-quart (3 L) saucepan, combine butter and chocolate. Melt over low heat, stirring constantly. Remove from heat. Cool slightly. Stir in 2 cups (500 mL) sugar and the liqueur. Add eggs, one at a time, beating after each addition. Add flour, baking powder and salt. Stir until well blended. Spread batter evenly in prepared pan. Set aside.

In small mixing bowl, combine filling ingredients. Beat at medium speed of electric mixer until smooth. Pour filling evenly over batter. Drop preserves by tablespoons onto filling to form 10 dollops.

Swirl filling and preserves through batter with table knife to marble. Bake for 45 to 50 minutes, or until wooden pick inserted in center comes out clean. Cool completely before cutting.

Choco-Mint Brownies

　1　cup (250 mL) butter or margarine
　4　squares (1 oz./30 g each) unsweetened baking
　　　chocolate
　2　cups (500 mL) sugar
½　teaspoon (2 mL) peppermint extract
　4　eggs
1⅓　cups (325 mL) all-purpose flour
¼　teaspoon (1 mL) salt
　1　cup (250 mL) mint-flavored chocolate chips
　1　cup (250 mL) semisweet chocolate chips

Glaze:
　1　square (1 oz./30 g) white baking chocolate
　1　teaspoon (5 mL) vegetable oil

32 brownies

Heat oven to 350°F (180°C). Lightly grease 13 x 9-inch (3.5 L) baking pan. Set aside. In 3-quart (3 L) saucepan, combine butter and unsweetened chocolate. Melt over medium heat, stirring constantly. Remove from heat. Cool slightly. Stir in sugar and peppermint extract. Add eggs, one at a time, beating after each addition. Add flour and salt. Stir until well blended.

Spread mixture evenly in prepared pan. Bake for 25 to 35 minutes, or until wooden pick inserted in center comes out clean. Immediately sprinkle with chips. Bake for additional 1 minute. Immediately spread melted chips evenly over brownies. In 1-quart (1 L) saucepan, combine glaze ingredients. Melt over low heat, stirring constantly.

Drizzle glaze in crosswise parallel lines 1 inch (2.5 cm) apart over top of melted chips. Immediately draw table knife lengthwise through glaze in straight lines to form pattern. Let dry completely before cutting.

Rocky Road Brownies (top)

1 cup (250 mL) butter or margarine
4 squares (1 oz./30 g each) unsweetened baking chocolate
2 cups (500 mL) granulated sugar
1 teaspoon (5 mL) vanilla
4 eggs
1 1/3 cups (325 mL) all-purpose flour
1/4 teaspoon (1 mL) salt
3 cups (750 mL) miniature marshmallows
1 cup (250 mL) salted peanuts

Glaze:

2 tablespoons (25 mL) butter or margarine
1 square (1 oz./30 g) unsweetened baking chocolate
1 cup (250 mL) powdered sugar
2 to 4 teaspoons (10 to 20 mL) milk

24 brownies

Heat oven to 350°F (180°C). Lightly grease 13 x 9-inch (3.5 L) baking pan. Set aside. In 3-quart (3 L) saucepan, combine 1 cup (250 mL) butter and 4 squares chocolate. Melt over low heat, stirring constantly. Remove from heat. Cool slightly. Stir in granulated sugar and vanilla. Add eggs, one at a time, beating after each addition. Add flour and salt. Stir until well blended.

Spread mixture evenly in prepared pan. Bake for 23 to 28 minutes, or until wooden pick inserted in center comes out clean. Immediately sprinkle marshmallows and peanuts evenly over brownies. Bake for additional 2 to 3 minutes, or until marshmallows are light golden brown. Set aside.

In 1-quart (1 L) saucepan, combine 2 tablespoons (25 mL) butter and 1 square chocolate. Melt over low heat, stirring constantly. Remove from heat. Add powdered sugar and milk. Stir until smooth. Drizzle glaze over marshmallows and peanuts.

Vanilla Frosted Brownies (bottom)

1 cup (250 mL) granulated sugar
2/3 cup (150 mL) butter or margarine
2 tablespoons (25 mL) milk
2 cups (500 mL) semisweet chocolate chips, divided
2 teaspoons (10 mL) vanilla
4 eggs
1 1/3 cups (325 mL) all-purpose flour
1/2 teaspoon (2 mL) baking powder
1/2 teaspoon (2 mL) salt
1/2 cup (125 mL) chopped pecans

Frosting (optional):

1 cup (250 mL) vanilla baking chips
1 tablespoon (15 mL) vegetable oil
2 cups (500 mL) powdered sugar
1/4 cup (50 mL) butter or margarine, melted
2 tablespoons (25 mL) water

32 brownies

Heat oven to 350°F (180°C). Lightly grease 13 x 9-inch (3.5 L) baking pan. Set aside. In 3-quart (3 L) saucepan, combine granulated sugar, 2/3 cup (150 mL) butter and the milk. Bring to boil over medium heat, stirring constantly. Remove from heat. Add 1 cup (250 mL) chocolate chips and the vanilla. Stir until chips are melted. Add eggs, one at a time, beating after each addition. Add flour, baking powder and salt. Stir until well blended. Stir in remaining 1 cup (250 mL) chocolate chips and the pecans.

Spread mixture evenly in prepared pan. Bake for 25 to 30 minutes, or until wooden pick inserted in center comes out clean. Cool completely.

In 1-quart (1 L) saucepan, combine vanilla chips and oil. Melt over low heat, stirring constantly. Remove from heat. Set aside. In medium mixing bowl, combine remaining frosting ingredients. Beat at low speed of electric mixer until smooth. Add melted chips. Beat at medium speed until smooth. Spread frosting evenly over brownies.

Crunchy Date Blondies

1¼ cups (300 mL) packed brown sugar
½ cup (125 mL) butter or margarine, softened
2 eggs
2 teaspoons (10 mL) vanilla
1½ cups (375 mL) all-purpose flour
1 teaspoon (5 mL) baking powder
¼ teaspoon (1 mL) salt
1 cup (250 mL) chopped dates
½ cup (125 mL) chopped pecans

Topping:
½ cup (125 mL) packed brown sugar
2 tablespoons (25 mL) butter or margarine, melted
2 tablespoons (25 mL) light corn syrup
2 tablespoons (25 mL) milk
1 cup (250 mL) flaked coconut
½ cup (125 mL) chopped pecans

32 brownies

Heat oven to 350°F (180°C). Lightly grease 13 x 9-inch (3.5 L) baking pan. Set aside. In large mixing bowl, combine 1¼ cups (300 mL) brown sugar and ½ cup (125 mL) butter. Beat at medium speed of electric mixer until light and fluffy. Add eggs and vanilla. Beat at medium speed until well blended. Add flour, baking powder and salt. Beat at low speed until well blended. Stir in dates and ½ cup (125 mL) pecans.

Spread mixture evenly in prepared pan. Bake for 20 to 28 minutes, or until golden brown. Remove from oven. Set oven to broil.

In medium mixing bowl, combine all topping ingredients, except coconut and pecans. Stir until well blended. Stir in coconut and ½ cup (125 mL) pecans. Spread topping evenly over brownies. Place under broiler, with surface of topping 4 inches (10 cm) from heat. Broil for 1 to 2 minutes, or until topping is bubbly. Cool completely before cutting.

Bars & Brownies

Rumba Brownies

1 cup (250 mL) granulated sugar
1/2 cup (125 mL) butter or margarine, softened
1 1/4 cups (300 mL) chocolate-flavored syrup
3 eggs
2 teaspoons (10 mL) rum extract
1 1/4 cups (300 mL) all-purpose flour
1 cup (250 mL) raisins
1/2 cup (125 mL) flaked coconut

Frosting:
1/4 cup (50 mL) butter or margarine
1/4 cup (50 mL) unsweetened cocoa
1 1/2 cups (375 mL) powdered sugar
2 to 3 tablespoons (25 to 50 mL) milk
1/4 teaspoon (1 mL) rum extract

32 brownies

Heat oven to 350°F (180°C). Lightly grease 13 x 9-inch (3.5 L) baking pan. Set aside. In large mixing bowl, combine granulated sugar and 1/2 cup (125 mL) butter. Beat at medium speed of electric mixer until light and fluffy. Add syrup, eggs and 2 teaspoons (10 mL) rum extract. Beat at low speed until well blended. Add flour. Beat at low speed until well blended. Stir in raisins and coconut.

Spread mixture evenly in prepared pan. Bake for 30 to 35 minutes, or until wooden pick inserted in center comes out clean. Cool completely.

In 2-quart (2 L) saucepan, melt 1/4 cup (50 mL) butter over medium heat. Stir in cocoa. Bring to boil, stirring constantly. Remove from heat. Cool slightly. Add remaining frosting ingredients. Stir until smooth. Spread frosting evenly over brownies.

Coffee Toffee Bars

1/2 cup (125 mL) sliced almonds
1 teaspoon (5 mL) instant coffee crystals
1 teaspoon (5 mL) hot water
2 cups (500 mL) all-purpose flour
1 cup (250 mL) packed brown sugar
3/4 cup (175 mL) butter or margarine, softened
1 egg
1/2 teaspoon (2 mL) baking soda
1/4 teaspoon (1 mL) salt
1 pkg. (6 oz./170 g) toffee chip bits
2 cups (500 mL) semisweet chocolate chips

50 bars

Heat oven to 350°F (180°C). Place almonds in 8-inch (2 L) square baking pan. Bake for 5 to 7 minutes, or until light golden brown, stirring twice. Set aside.

In small bowl, combine coffee crystals and water. Stir until crystals are dissolved. In large mixing bowl, combine coffee, flour, sugar, butter, egg, baking soda and salt. Beat at medium speed of electric mixer until soft dough forms. Stir in toffee bits.

Press dough evenly into ungreased 15 1/2 x 10 1/2-inch (40 x 25 cm) jelly roll pan. Bake for 15 to 20 minutes, or until golden brown. Immediately sprinkle with chocolate chips. Bake for additional 1 minute. Immediately spread melted chips evenly over bars. Sprinkle toasted almonds evenly over chocolate. Cool completely before cutting.

Deluxe Crispy Bars

1 pkg. (10 oz./ 283 g) vanilla baking chips
1 cup (250 mL) creamy peanut butter
4 cups (1 L) crisp rice cereal
1 cup (250 mL) Spanish peanuts

16 bars

Lightly grease 8-inch (2 L) square baking pan. Set aside. In 2-quart (2 L) saucepan, melt chips over low heat, stirring constantly. Add peanut butter. Stir until smooth. Add cereal and peanuts. Stir to coat. Press mixture evenly into prepared pan. Chill until set before cutting.

Bars & Brownies

Hawaiian Brownies (top)

1/2 cup (125 mL) granulated sugar
1/3 cup (75 mL) butter or margarine
1 can (8¼ oz./234 g) crushed pineapple in juice,
    well drained (reserve 2 tablespoons/25 mL
    juice)
1 cup (250 mL) semisweet chocolate chips
1/2 teaspoon (2 mL) rum extract
2 eggs
1 cup (250 mL) all-purpose flour
1/2 cup (125 mL) flaked coconut
1/2 teaspoon (2 mL) baking powder
1/4 teaspoon (1 mL) salt

Frosting:

2 cups (500 mL) powdered sugar
1 pkg. (3 oz./85 g) cream cheese, softened
1 to 2 tablespoons (15 to 25 mL) milk
1/4 teaspoon (1 mL) rum extract
1/2 cup (125 mL) chopped pecans

16 brownies

Heat oven to 350°F (180°C). Lightly grease 8-inch (2 L) square baking pan. Set aside. In 2-quart (2 L) saucepan, combine granulated sugar, butter and reserved juice. Bring to boil over medium heat, stirring constantly. Remove from heat. Add chips and 1/2 teaspoon (2 mL) rum extract. Stir until smooth. Add eggs, one at a time, beating after each addition. Add pineapple, flour, coconut, baking powder and salt. Stir until well blended.

Spread mixture evenly in prepared pan. Bake for 25 to 30 minutes, or until wooden pick inserted in center comes out clean. Cool completely.

In medium mixing bowl, combine all frosting ingredients, except pecans. Beat at low speed of electric mixer until smooth. Stir in pecans. Spread frosting evenly over brownies.

Raspberry Bars with Lemon Icing (bottom)

3 cups (750 mL) all-purpose flour
1½ cups (375 mL) granulated sugar
1/2 teaspoon (2 mL) baking soda
1/2 teaspoon (2 mL) grated lemon peel
1 cup (250 mL) butter or margarine, chilled
1 egg, slightly beaten

Filling:

1 pkg. (12 oz./341 g) frozen lightly sweetened
    raspberries
1¼ cups (300 mL) granulated sugar
1/4 cup (50 mL) water
3 tablespoons (50 mL) cornstarch
1/2 teaspoon (2 mL) grated lemon peel
1/2 teaspoon (2 mL) vanilla

Icing:

1¼ cups (300 mL) powdered sugar
1 to 2 tablespoons (15 to 25 mL) fresh lemon
    juice
1 tablespoon (15 mL) butter or margarine, softened

32 bars

Heat oven to 350°F (180°C). In large mixing bowl, combine flour, 1½ cups (375 mL) granulated sugar, the baking soda and 1/2 teaspoon (2 mL) peel. Using pastry blender, cut in chilled butter and the egg until mixture resembles coarse crumbs. Reserve 2 cups (500 mL) flour mixture. Press remaining flour mixture evenly into ungreased 15½ x 10½-inch (40 x 25 cm) jelly roll pan to form base. Bake for 8 minutes.

In 2-quart (2 L) saucepan, combine filling ingredients. Cook over medium-high heat until raspberries are defrosted and filling is thickened, stirring frequently. Spread filling evenly over base. Sprinkle reserved flour mixture evenly over filling. Bake for additional 15 to 20 minutes, or until golden brown. Cool slightly.

In small mixing bowl, combine icing ingredients. Stir until smooth. Drizzle icing over warm bars. Cool completely before cutting.

Gooey Mixed Nut Bars

1½ cups (375 mL) all-purpose
   flour
¾ cup (175 mL) packed brown
   sugar
½ teaspoon (2 mL) salt
½ cup (125 mL) plus 1
   tablespoon (15 mL) butter or
   margarine, chilled, divided
 1 cup (250 mL) butterscotch
   chips
½ cup (125 mL) light corn
   syrup
 1 can (12 oz./341 g) salted
   mixed nuts

30 bars

Heat oven to 350°F (180°C). In
medium mixing bowl, combine
flour, sugar and salt. Using
pastry blender, cut in ½ cup
(125 mL) butter until mixture
resembles coarse crumbs. Press
mixture evenly into ungreased
11 x 7-inch (2 L) baking pan to
form base. Bake for 15 to 18
minutes, or until edges are
light golden brown.

In 2-quart (2 L) saucepan, combine remaining 1 tablespoon
(15 mL) butter, the chips and
corn syrup. Cook over medium
heat until chips are melted,
stirring constantly. Remove
from heat. Stir in nuts. Spread
mixture evenly over base.
Bake for additional 10 to 15
minutes, or until edges are
bubbly. Cool completely
before cutting.

Toffee Bit Blondies

1 cup (250 mL) *packed brown sugar*

½ cup (125 mL) *butter or margarine, softened*

2 *eggs*

2 *teaspoons (10 mL) vanilla*

1½ *cups (375 mL) all-purpose flour*

1 *teaspoon (5 mL) baking powder*

¼ *teaspoon (1 mL) salt*

½ *cup (125 mL) miniature semisweet chocolate chips*

½ *cup (125 mL) English toffee bits*
Powdered sugar

32 brownies

Heat oven to 350°F (180°C). Lightly grease 13 × 9-inch (3.5 L) baking pan. Set aside. In large mixing bowl, combine sugar and butter. Beat at medium speed of electric mixer until light and fluffy. Add eggs and vanilla. Beat at medium speed until well blended. Add flour, baking powder and salt. Beat at low speed until well blended. Stir in bits.

Spread mixture evenly in prepared pan. Bake for 23 to 28 minutes, or until wooden pick inserted in center comes out clean. Cool completely. Sprinkle brownies evenly with powdered sugar.

No-bake Peanut Butter Bars

  2 *cups (500 mL) graham cracker crumbs*
1½ *cups (375 mL) powdered sugar*
  1 *cup (250 mL) chunky peanut butter*
  ½ *cup (125 mL) butter or margarine, melted*
  ½ *cup (125 mL) chopped salted peanuts*
1½ *cups (375 mL) milk chocolate chips*

30 bars

Lightly grease 11 x 7-inch (2 L) baking pan. Set aside. In large mixing bowl, combine all ingredients, except chips. Press mixture evenly into prepared pan.

In 1-quart (1 L) saucepan, melt chips over low heat, stirring constantly. Spread chocolate evenly over bars. Chill until set before cutting.

Microwave tip: In medium mixing bowl, melt chips at 50% (Medium) for 2½ to 5½ minutes, stirring after every minute. Continue as directed.

Bars & Brownies

Honey Oat Peanut Bars

  7 cups (1.75 L) honey graham round oat cereal
1¼ cups (300 mL) honey-roasted peanuts
1½ cups (375 mL) light corn syrup
  1 cup (250 mL) granulated sugar
  1 cup (250 mL) packed brown sugar
  1 cup (250 mL) creamy honey-roasted peanut
     butter

50 bars

Lightly grease 15½ x 10½-inch (40 x 25 cm) jelly roll pan. Set aside. In large mixing bowl, combine cereal and peanuts. Set cereal mixture aside.

In 3-quart (3 L) saucepan, combine corn syrup and sugars. Bring to boil over high heat, stirring occasionally. Boil for 1 minute. Remove from heat. Add peanut butter. Stir until smooth.

Pour syrup mixture over cereal mixture. Stir to coat. Press mixture evenly into prepared pan. Chill until set before cutting.

Bars & Brownies

Double Caramel Bars

32 caramels
½ cup (125 mL) half-and-half
1 cup (250 mL) uncooked
   multigrain hot cereal
1 cup (250 mL) all-purpose
   flour
¾ cup (175 mL) packed brown
   sugar
½ teaspoon (2 mL) baking soda
¼ teaspoon (1 mL) salt
¾ cup (175 mL) butter or
   margarine, chilled
½ cup (125 mL) semisweet
   chocolate chips
½ cup (125 mL) butterscotch
   chips
½ cup (125 mL) chopped
   pecans

32 bars

Heat oven to 350°F (180°C). In 2-quart (2 L) saucepan, combine caramels and half-and-half. Cook over medium-low heat until smooth, stirring constantly. Remove from heat. Set caramel mixture aside.

In large mixing bowl, combine cereal, flour, sugar, baking soda and salt. Using pastry blender, cut in butter until mixture resembles coarse crumbs. Reserve 1 cup (250 mL) cereal mixture.

Press remaining cereal mixture evenly into ungreased 13 x 9-inch (3.5 L) baking pan to form base. Bake for 10 minutes. Immediately pour caramel mixture evenly over base.

Sprinkle chips and pecans evenly over caramel mixture. Sprinkle reserved cereal mixture evenly over chips and pecans. Bake for additional 15 to 18 minutes, or until golden brown. Cool completely before cutting.

Almond Coconut Bars

2 cups (500 mL) chocolate
  cookie crumbs
1/2 cup (125 mL) butter or
  margarine, melted
1/4 cup (50 mL) sugar

Filling:
2 cups (500 mL) flaked coconut
1 can (14 oz./396 g) sweetened
  condensed milk
1/2 cup (125 mL) chopped
  almonds

1 cup (250 mL) semisweet
  chocolate chips
1 cup (250 mL) milk chocolate
  chips

30 bars

Heat oven to 350°F (180°C). In medium mixing bowl, combine crumbs, butter and sugar. Press evenly into ungreased 11 x 7-inch (2 L) baking pan to form base. Bake for 10 minutes. Cool completely.

In second medium mixing bowl, combine filling ingredients. Spread filling evenly over base. Bake for additional 18 to 20 minutes, or until edges are light golden brown. (Filling will set as it cools.) Cool completely.

In 1-quart (1 L) saucepan, melt chips over low heat, stirring constantly. Spread melted chips evenly over bars. Chill until set before cutting. Store in refrigerator.

Microwave tip: In medium mixing bowl, melt chips at 50% (Medium) for 2 1/2 to 5 1/2 minutes, stirring after every minute. Continue as directed.

Cranberry Pumpkin Bars

  2 cups (500 mL) all-purpose
      flour
  2 cups (500 mL) granulated
      sugar
  1 can (16 oz./454 g) pumpkin
  1 cup (250 mL) vegetable oil
  4 eggs
  2 teaspoons (10 mL) baking
      powder
1½ teaspoons (7 mL) ground
      cinnamon
  1 teaspoon (5 mL) baking soda
  ½ teaspoon (2 mL) salt
  ¾ cup (175 mL) dried
      cranberries
  ½ cup (125 mL) chopped pecans

Frosting:
  3 tablespoons (50 ml) butter
      or margarine
  3 cups (750 mL) powdered
      sugar
  3 to 4 tablespoons (50 mL) milk
  1 teaspoon (5 mL) vanilla

50 bars

Heat oven to 350°F (180°C).
Lightly grease 15½ × 10½-
inch (40 × 25 cm) jelly roll pan.
Set aside. In large mixing bowl,
combine flour, granulated sugar,
pumpkin, oil, eggs, baking powder, cinnamon, baking soda and
salt. Beat at medium speed of
electric mixer until well blended.
Stir in cranberries and pecans.

Spread mixture evenly in
prepared pan. Bake for 23 to
25 minutes, or until slight impression remains when bars
are lightly touched in center.
Cool completely.

In 2-quart (2 L) saucepan, cook
butter over medium heat until
light golden brown. Remove
from heat. Add remaining
frosting ingredients. Stir until
smooth. Spread frosting evenly
over bars.

Chocolate Chip Banana Bars

½ cup (125 mL) granulated
    sugar
½ cup (125 mL) packed brown
    sugar
½ cup (125 mL) vegetable
    shortening
2 eggs
1½ cups (375 mL) all-purpose
    flour
1 cup (250 mL) mashed
    bananas (2 medium)
½ teaspoon (2 mL) baking powder
½ teaspoon (2 mL) baking soda
½ teaspoon (2 mL) salt
¾ cup (175 mL) miniature
    semisweet chocolate chips

Frosting:

¾ cup (175 mL) powdered sugar
½ cup (125 mL) semisweet
    chocolate chips, melted and
    slightly cooled
2 to 3 tablespoons (25 to 50 mL)
    milk
2 tablespoons (25 mL) butter
    or margarine, softened
½ teaspoon (2 mL) vanilla

32 bars

Heat oven to 350°F (180°C).
Lightly grease 13 x 9-inch (3.5 L)
baking pan. Set aside. In large
mixing bowl, combine granulated sugar, brown sugar,
shortening and eggs. Beat at
medium speed of electric mixer
until light and fluffy. Add flour,
bananas, baking powder,
baking soda and salt. Beat at
low speed until well blended.
Stir in miniature chips.

Spread batter evenly in prepared pan. Bake for 20 to 25
minutes, or until slight impression remains when bars are
lightly touched in center. Cool
completely.

In small mixing bowl, combine frosting ingredients. Beat
at low speed of electric mixer
until smooth. Spread frosting
evenly over bars.

Hazelnut Blondies (top)

 1/2 *cup (125 mL) chopped hazelnuts*
   1 *cup (250 mL) granulated sugar*
 1/2 *cup (125 mL) packed brown sugar*
 1/2 *cup (125 mL) butter or margarine, softened*
   2 *eggs*
   2 *tablespoons (25 mL) hazelnut liqueur*
1 1/2 *cups (375 mL) all-purpose flour*
   1 *teaspoon (5 mL) baking powder*
 1/2 *teaspoon (2 mL) salt*

Frosting:
   2 *tablespoons (25 mL) butter or margarine*
   2 *cups (500 mL) powdered sugar*
   2 *to 3 tablespoons (25 to 50 mL) milk*
   1 *tablespoon (15 mL) hazelnut liqueur*

32 brownies

Heat oven to 350°F (180°C). Lightly grease 13 x 9-inch (3.5 L) baking pan. Set aside. Place hazelnuts in 8-inch (2 L) square baking pan. Bake for 7 to 9 minutes, or just until nuts begin to brown, stirring twice. Set aside.

In large mixing bowl, combine granulated sugar, brown sugar, and 1/2 cup (125 mL) butter. Beat at medium speed of electric mixer until light and fluffy. Add eggs and 2 tablespoons (25 mL) liqueur. Beat at low speed until well blended. Add flour, baking powder and salt. Beat at low speed until well blended. Stir in hazelnuts.

Spread mixture evenly in prepared pan. Bake for 20 to 25 minutes, or until wooden pick inserted in center comes out clean. Cool completely.

In 1-quart (1 L) saucepan, cook 2 tablespoons (25 mL) butter over medium heat until light golden brown. Remove from heat. Add remaining frosting ingredients. Stir until smooth. Spread frosting evenly over brownies.

Chocolate-covered Cherry Bars (bottom)

   1 *cup (250 mL) all-purpose flour*
 1/2 *cup (125 mL) butter or margarine, softened*
 1/4 *cup (50 mL) granulated sugar*
   2 *tablespoons (25 mL) unsweetened cocoa*

Fondant:
   2 *cups (500 mL) powdered sugar*
   2 *tablespoons (25 mL) butter or margarine, softened*
   2 *tablespoons (25 mL) half-and-half or milk*
 1/4 *teaspoon (1 mL) almond extract*

  36 *red maraschino cherries, well drained*
   1 *cup (250 mL) semisweet chocolate chips*
   1 *teaspoon (5 mL) vegetable shortening*

36 bars

Heat oven to 350°F (180°C). In medium mixing bowl, combine flour, 1/2 cup (125 mL) butter, the granulated sugar and cocoa. Beat at low speed of electric mixer until soft dough forms. Press mixture evenly into ungreased 8-inch (2 L) square baking pan to form base. Bake for 15 to 18 minutes, or until set. Cool completely.

In second medium mixing bowl, combine fondant ingredients. Beat at low speed until smooth. Carefully spread fondant evenly over base. Arrange cherries over fondant in 6 rows of 6.

In 1-quart (1 L) saucepan, combine chips and shortening. Melt over low heat, stirring constantly. Spoon melted chips over and between cherries, spreading to cover fondant. Chill until set before cutting. Store in refrigerator.

Microwave tip: In small mixing bowl, melt chips and shortening at 50% (Medium) for 2 1/2 to 5 minutes, stirring after every minute. Continue as directed.

Orange Rhubarb Bars

Filling:

  1 *pkg. (16 oz./454 g) frozen unsweetened rhubarb*
1½ *cups (375 mL) granulated sugar*
  ¼ *cup (50 mL) water*
  2 *tablespoons (25 mL) cornstarch*
  1 *teaspoon (5 mL) vanilla*
  3 *to 4 drops red food coloring*

1½ *cups (375 mL) uncooked multigrain hot cereal*
1½ *cups (375 mL) all-purpose flour*
  1 *cup (250 mL) packed brown sugar*
  ½ *teaspoon (2 mL) baking soda*
  ½ *teaspoon (2 mL) grated orange peel*
  1 *cup (250 mL) butter or margarine, chilled*
  ½ *cup (125 mL) chopped pecans*

24 bars

Heat oven to 375°F (190°C). Lightly grease 13 x 9-inch (3.5 L) baking pan. Set aside. In 3-quart (3 L) saucepan, combine all filling ingredients, except food coloring. Cook over medium-high heat until rhubarb is defrosted and filling is thickened and transucent, stirring constantly. Remove from heat. Stir in food coloring. Set aside.

In large mixing bowl, combine cereal, flour, brown sugar, baking soda and peel. Using pastry blender, cut in butter until mixture resembles coarse crumbs. Reserve 1½ cups (375 mL) cereal mixture.

Press remaining cereal mixture evenly into prepared pan to form base. Spread filling evenly over base. Sprinkle reserved cereal mixture and pecans evenly over filling. Bake for 20 to 25 minutes, or until golden brown. Cool completely before cutting.

Fudgy Cashew Brownies

1 cup (250 mL) granulated
   sugar
1/2 cup (125 mL) butter or
   margarine, softened
2 eggs
1/3 cup (75 mL) unsweetened
   cocoa
1 teaspoon (5 mL) vanilla
1 1/4 cups (300 mL) all-purpose
   flour
1/2 teaspoon (2 mL) baking soda
1/4 teaspoon (1 mL) salt
1/2 cup (125 mL) chopped
   cashews

Frosting:
2 cups (500 mL) powdered sugar
2 to 4 tablespoons (25 to 50 mL)
   milk
2 tablespoons (25 mL) butter
   or margarine, softened
1/2 teaspoon (2 mL) vanilla

1/3 cup (75 mL) cashew halves

16 brownies

Heat oven to 350°F (180°C).
Lightly grease 8-inch (2 L)
square baking pan. Set aside.
In large mixing bowl, combine
granulated sugar and 1/2 cup
(125 mL) butter. Beat at medium
speed of electric mixer until
light and fluffy. Add eggs, cocoa
and vanilla. Beat at medium
speed until well blended. Add
flour, baking soda and salt. Beat
at low speed until well blended.
Stir in chopped cashews.

Spread mixture evenly in prepared pan. Bake for 23 to 33
minutes, or until wooden pick
inserted in center comes out
clean. (Do not overbake.) Cool
completely.

In medium mixing bowl, combine frosting ingredients. Beat
at low speed of electric mixer
until smooth. Spread frosting
evenly over brownies. Sprinkle
cashew halves evenly over
frosting.

Bars & Brownies

Lemon Cheesecake Bars

1³/₄ cups (425 mL) crushed vanilla wafers
 ¹/₂ cup (125 mL) butter or margarine, melted
  2 tablespoons (25 mL) sugar

Filling:
  1 pkg. (8 oz./227 g) cream cheese, softened
 ¹/₃ cup (75 mL) sugar
 ¹/₂ cup (125 mL) sour cream
  1 egg
1¹/₂ teaspoons (7 mL) grated lemon peel
  1 teaspoon (5 mL) vanilla

 ¹/₄ cup (50 mL) seedless raspberry preserves,
     melted

16 bars

Heat oven to 350°F (180°C). In small mixing bowl, combine wafers, butter and 2 tablespoons (25 mL) sugar. Press evenly into ungreased 8-inch (2 L) square baking pan to form base. Set aside.

In medium mixing bowl, combine cream cheese and ¹/₃ cup (75 mL) sugar. Beat at medium speed of electric mixer until smooth. Add remaining filling ingredients. Beat at medium speed until well blended.

Spread filling evenly over base. Bake for 50 to 55 minutes, or until light golden brown. Cool completely. Drizzle preserves over bars. Store in refrigerator.

Bars & Brownies

Carrot-Date Bars

    1   cup (250 mL) all-purpose flour
    1   cup (250 mL) granulated sugar
  3/4   cup (175 mL) vegetable oil
    2   eggs
  1/2   teaspoon (2 mL) baking soda
  1/2   teaspoon (2 mL) ground cinnamon
  1/2   teaspoon (2 mL) ground cloves
  1/2   teaspoon (2 mL) salt
1 1/2   cups (375 mL) grated carrots
  1/2   cup (125 mL) chopped dates
        Powdered sugar

Heat oven to 350°F (180°C). In large mixing bowl, combine flour, granulated sugar, oil, eggs, baking soda, cinnamon, cloves and salt. Beat at medium speed of electric mixer until well blended. Stir in carrots and dates.

Spread mixture evenly in ungreased 13 x 9-inch (3.5 L) baking pan. Bake for 28 to 32 minutes, or until wooden pick inserted in center comes out clean. Cool completely. Sprinkle bars evenly with powdered sugar.

24 bars

Decorating Cookies

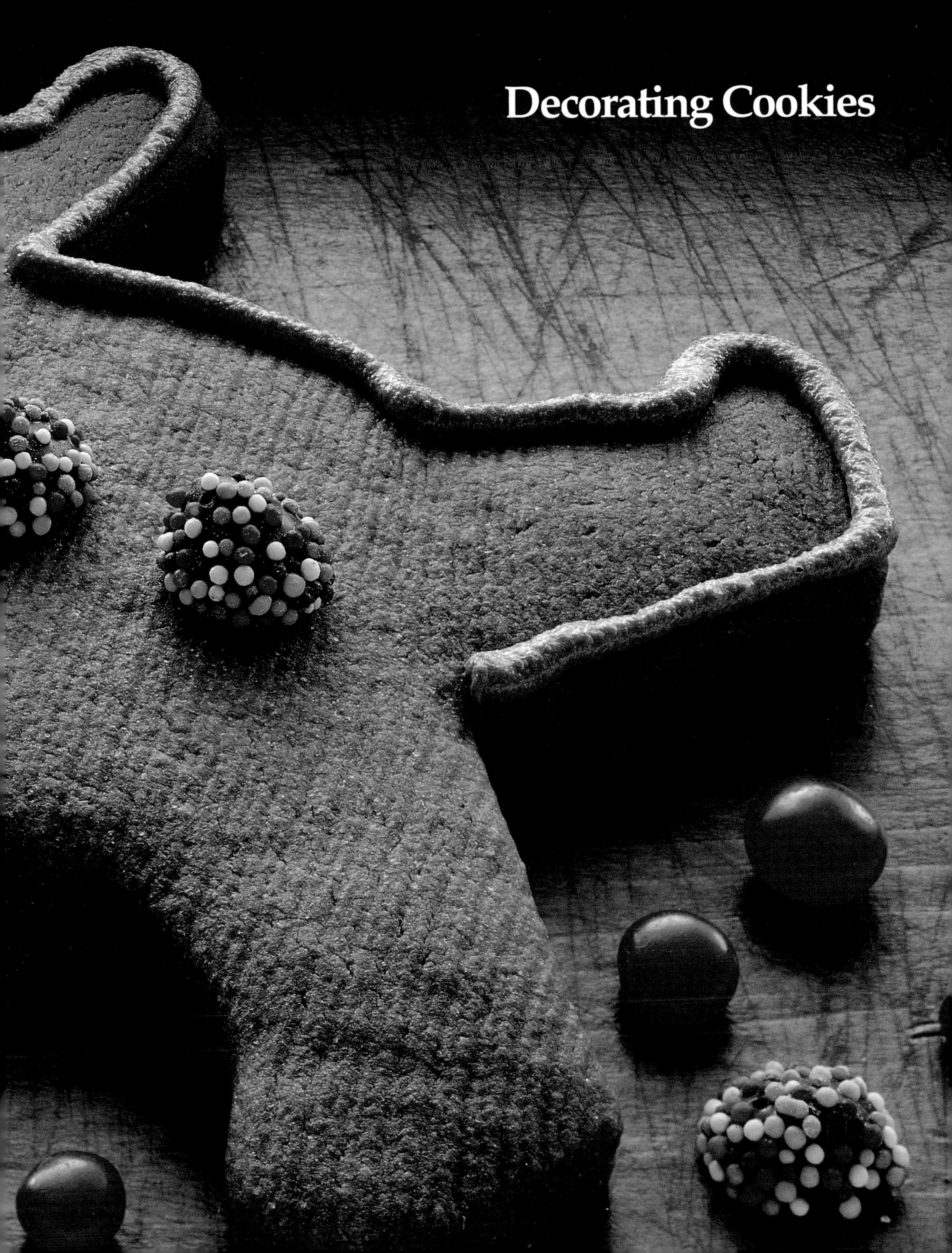

Decorating with Frosting

The quickest and easiest way to decorate cookies is with frosting. Here is a recipe for a basic decorator frosting that can be used for spreading or piping on cookies.

Decorator Frosting

¹/₂ cup (125 mL) butter or margarine, softened
¹/₂ cup (125 mL) vegetable shortening
1 teaspoon (5 mL) vanilla
4 cups (1 L) powered sugar
3 to 4 tablespoons (50 mL) milk
　Food coloring (optional)

3 cups (750 mL)

In large mixing bowl, combine butter, shortening and vanilla. Beat at medium speed of electric mixer until creamy. Add sugar, 1 cup (250 mL) at a time, beating at low speed until well blended. Add milk. Beat at medium speed until light and fluffy. Beat in food coloring, 1 drop at a time, until frosting is desired color.

Tip: One-half teaspoon (2 mL) almond extract, mint extract or other flavored extract can be substituted for vanilla.

Use a small frosting spatula or table knife to spread frosting evenly on cookies. (Do not spread frosting too thick.) Frost cookies that are completely cooled, so the frosting does not melt. Also, warm cookies are more fragile and might break during the handling that is required.

Thin frosting by beating in milk, 1 tablespoon (15 mL) at a time (for small amounts, ¹/₂ teaspoon/2 mL at a time), until desired consistency.

Drizzle thinned frosting over the cookies with a spoon.

Decorating Cookies

Dip corner or part of cookie in slightly thinned frosting. If desired, sprinkle with chopped nuts, coconut or other decorative topping (see page 250). Cookies can also be dipped in melted chocolate or vanilla chips, or in melted candy coating.

Paint thinned frosting on cookies for a detailed look, or use a paintbrush to make designs and textures in frosting.

Pull fork tines through lines of frosting to create a marbled look.

Place stencil over freshly frosted cookie, and lightly dust with sifted powdered sugar.

Decorating Cookies

Decorating with a Pastry Bag

Use a pastry bag to pipe frosting on cookies. These bags are available at specialty kitchen stores and some supermarkets. Inexpensive metal or plastic decorating tips are also available at these stores. A coupler allows you to change decorating tips without emptying the pastry bag.

Pictured are six of the more common decorating tips.

#2 Writing tip

#5 Writing tip

#67 Leaf tip

#13 Open star tip

#27 Closed star tip

#18 Open star tip

How to Use a Pastry Bag

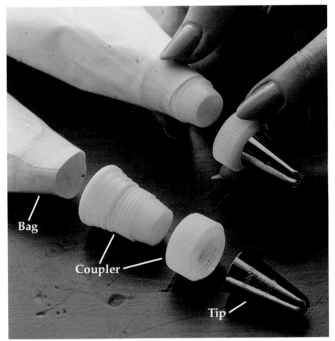

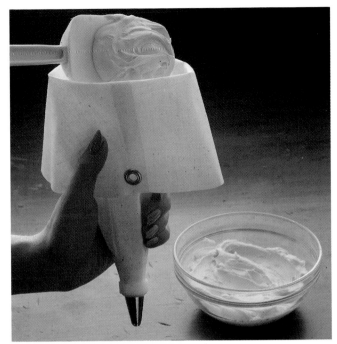

1) Place large part of coupler in bag, making sure bag fits snugly around coupler. Place tip through small part of coupler, then screw both halves of coupler together.

2) Scoop frosting into rolled-down pastry bag until bag is about two-thirds full. (Roll up bag while filling.)

How to Make a Pastry Bag

3) Twist or roll down the top of the bag to keep steady pressure on the frosting as you squeeze. Before decorating, hold the bag closed and squeeze out a small amount of frosting to eliminate air bubbles in the bag.

Fill a heavy, resealable food-storage bag half full of frosting; seal the bag. Snip off the tip (arrow) of one corner to create a writing tip that produces a line. Start with a small hole, and enlarge it, if necessary. A coupler and decorating tips can also be used with food-storage bags.

Decorative Toppings

Decorative toppings can be sprinkled over or pressed on frostings, as shown below. Add toppings to cookies before frosting dries, so toppings will stay in place. Or put toppings on cookies before baking, and leave the cookies unfrosted. Toppings like dried fruit, candies or nuts can sometimes be pressed into cookies fresh from the oven.

Colored sugar is tinted granulated sugar and is available in several colors and granule sizes.

Decorating or coarse sugar has granules about four times larger than those of regular granulated sugar. Dragées are tiny, round hard candies that come in sizes ranging from pinhead to 1/4-inch (5 mm). Shot, confetti and sprinkles are commonly available decorative toppings.

Candies, dried fruit, nuts, miniature chocolate chips, licorice, coconut and grated citrus peel can also be used as cookie toppings.

Gumdrops

Cinnamon candies

Dragées

Whole nuts

Candied fruits

Chopped nuts

Miniature chips

Candy-coated chocolate pieces

Shot

Colored sugar

Grated citrus peel

Confetti

Jelly beans

Sprinkles

Licorice

Coarse sugar

Shredded coconut

More
Decorating Ideas

Here are some additional ideas for decorating home-baked cookies or cookies you buy at the store:

Cut dried fruit, gumdrops and licorice strings to make designs, eyes, hats, etc.

Place a small amount of fairly stiff frosting or a gumdrop in a garlic press. Carefully press out strands for "hair" or a textured look.

Smooth thin frosting base on cookies. Let it dry, then pipe outline or design on top. Decorative toppings can be added to complete the design.

How to Tint Coconut

Color coconut by placing it in a large, resealable food-storage bag. Add a few drops of food color to get desired color.

Seal bag and shake until coconut is uniform in color. Spread coconut on wax paper and let stand for a few minutes before using.

Index